14 × 14

IAN MONK

TRANSLATED FROM THE FRENCH BY
PHILIP TERRY AND IAN MONK

Originally published in French by L'Âne Qui Butine, 2013. Some of the translations in the volume originally appeared, sometimes in a different form, in the Oulipo Supplement in *PN Review* 259 (May–June 2021) and in the chapbook *Interludes* (Ma Bibliothèque, 2021).

© 2024 by Ian Monk

All Rights Reserved.

Set in Mrs Eaves with LaTeX.

ISBN: 978-1-952386-77-0 (paperback)
Library of Congress Control Number: 2023949163

Sagging Meniscus Press
Montclair, New Jersey
saggingmeniscus.com

Contents

Prelude: Love Is Sketched Out — 1

1. Wherever — 2

Interlude: Orifices — 11

2. In Bourges — 13

Interlude: Listen Out — 22

3. No Matter — 24

Interlude: The Blues of a Real Loser — 32

4. At My Place I — 35

Interlude: Alice Slips — 44

5. On the Lille Metro — 46

Interlude: Filthy Time — 55

6. I Thought Everywhere — 57

Interlude: Forget It Never Mind (I) — 66

7. At My Place II	*68*
Interlude: But Now	*77*
8. I Thought Again	*79*
Interlude: The Insect Contemplating	*88*
9. On the Train	*90*
Interlude: The Paris of Clouds	*99*
10. At My Place III	*101*
Interlude: And You	*110*
11. Whichever the Café	*112*
Interlude: If I Were You	*121*
12. Whatever	*123*
Interlude: Songs of Reflections	*131*
13. Relative Redundancy	*133*
Interlude: Forget It Never Mind (2)	*142*
14. The End	*144*
Coda: By the Sea	*152*

14 × 14

Love Is Sketched Out

love is sketched out here to see
like a finger
telling the tale of a life
like a drunk
before falling silent at last
like a stiff

like two stiffs
stretched out by the sea
knowing how at last
our own fingers
like drunks
tell the tale of our lives

what starts up is life
as a future stiff
in a dancing cloud of drink
stretched out by the sea
by our fingers
knowing how at last

Wherever

Here for example why not while wait-
ing for elsewhere and having been somewhere else too
just recently in this ascent straight
towards wherever and anyhow leading to
needful things to fill in the time
your brains too or what's left of them dunno
as for me what's on the box tonight spare a dime
and what about going to a museum or the opera lo-
l?

    here time runs like through a canal full
of sludge popped footballs corpses intentional or not
with on the top an oil slick a dead gull
plus a fridge here time does not take wing as in grot
real poetrees not a bit of it at all it flows
like it's weeping here on the Deûle with time that goes
like who gives a fuck

                    what we are doing here
is taking up all our time which is rented out
unfurnished as new because it's quite clear
in a springtime pretty or not today we're all about
being an Odysseus so pleased with himself

14 × 14

hitchhiking back home at last changing nothing at all

time in its abstract sense and not yet put on the shelf
of relativity as brother or sister in a fall
why not into a still-free space
which doesn't fill up yet either cannot so easily
kill itself as all that how smooth its face
is like an ephebe as objectively empty
as those two whisky bottles back home

                                                        what we're thinking now
is just enough to get through a month again plough
on through a day another year yes while we're at it
with just enough to make it to the next parti-
cle of time that dark matter every bit
as fleeting but also at the same moment as weighty
as a flow of photons between you talking
and me listening mouth agape looking into the distance
of your seemingly solid eyes with your wrinkles walking
across your truly virtual existence
which you zigzag quite timely all around you
and that time makes progress like flocks
of crows' feet on your face

                                      meanwhile the boys in blue
struggle in their boat to dredge the water and rocks

of the Deûle while finding everything they're not looking for
a fine assortment of stiffs but not that of the daugh-
ter of the UMP parliamentary candidate van-
ished since a fortnight ago now (who's fine and dandy
by the way right now pissing her can after can
of Kro into the waterless crapper of a squat as ugly
and as sexy as her new geezer while
her dad suddenly feels ashamed (wow) when
he finds himself weighing up the pile
of sympathy votes he will probably then
get from a public moved by his loss
which has still to be confirmed but you can get
his sublime features toss-
ing between a dumb grin and the onset
of a flood of crocodile tears (suddenly
sincere) fuck it say the cops nothing doing then aquatically
backtracking towards the bank it's very soon
aperitif time down the station after all

so right in the Deûle no candidate's daughter (June)
(God be praised) but (it's crazy a tall
story but no need to dive into a lake beneath the Antarctic
that's been cut off for a million year-
s to find such an ecologic-
al system) but instead a kind of queer
grunge lab uniting human waste of all

14 × 14

kinds (organic or not) mingled up later
and macerated inside such a dung ball
coming from all the other non-human creator-
s for example to make for a new world of things
allergic to pure water without eyes or wings
drinking oil and eating phosphates that
deserve our protection just as much as baby
seals (studying their genes might be what
universally cures cancer who fucking knows) so be
damned this fucking anthropomorphism

                                                                                                          then
fuller of life than ever she comes back out of the bog
to join the others and the Kro apparently en-
dless so much the cans in the smog
the fags etcetera seem to be growing everywhere
all half full or else half empty
but never completely one or the other right there
it's a miracle like Jesus filling the five thousandth belly
with five little rolls and two or three sardines
no it's the water turning into plonk that's what she means
yes in vino veritas (she's done Latin at school all
the same) at the wedding of some bloke or other anyway
who gives a fuck she picks up a beer not cool
at all and plunges her body back into the dance

                                        two neighbours bray
for no apparent reason one of whom
is hanging around for no apparent reason on the pavement
in the moonlight surrounded by raucous music of doom
and confusion cut to pieces by the salient
shards of bottles still stuck there in the frame
of the only window still lit up
on rue Mirabeau then they calm down make lame
excuses to the cops who turn up
no problem officer yes I'll move on good night sir
nothing to do nothing to see

                             while footsteps then blur
away into the moonlight official fists hammer
on the door which is so frail that even if they had
the right key using it would be dumber
than fuck it snaps open immediately then inward pad
combat boots across the threshold

                                    in this dirty Deûle
of a life of accommodation of frequentations she
lets herself be cuffed and for now this lonely girl
sits looking at the moon from her cell she'd be free
in no time she knows if she mentioned her father
a skeleton key from right here and now but then
it'd be a padlocked bedroom so she'd rather

14 × 14

not return to her family home so silen-
ce patience everything ends up ending even hell
despite what the Catholics say those bell
wethers arse-fucked one by the others with outgrown
beliefs or a queer-boy not made so by his biological
dad who's been ordained to beat it all with a gown
covering his pendulous gut (a risk he wouldn't run at all
with two diesel-dike mums (without any
strap-ons (special prostate or not) just super
(which blasts to shit the idea that incongruity
is the theoretical basis of black or even white humour
(well yes, a few philosophy hours at the Uni Lille 3
as well (no one's perfect after all) if that is
you consider this to be humour[1]
at all) quite another way of taking the piss
another form (conic or not)) but you need to admit
it really when faced by two real dick-swingers) no it's shit
that's all that's all the two of them are equally crap alas
shut up then and play the sewn-up cunt

                                                the sun

rises on rue Mirabeau its fresh mass
of rubbish bags and its truck parked gun-
barrel straight in the middle of the street thus creating

---

[1] Like me (author's note)

the as yet modest beginnings of a traffic jam
they hoot and hoot their horns frustrating-
ly waking those still asleep more hoots the damn
cunt doesn't move someone gets out of their car to get
the crowbar from their boot and goes off to smash
that dickhead's face in as well a very long screwdriver bet-
ter than words to kick off a contradictory debate a lash-
ing of thoughts as done in any democratic country
with any self-respect just like France evidently
to cut it short for readers with a sensitive soul
(if any are left) under eyes that are half worried
half marvelling and quite clearly whol-
ly happy about any attempt conducted
by people never mind the colour of their skin
or the more or less frizzy nature of their hair
to enliven a little more this neighbourhood like a bin
going from bad to worse anyway right there
and then shortly after this contradictory debate
which was quite short and disappointing the dickhead
in question finally sets off blood on his pate
and in his eyes while our friend brandishes his slightly
red crowbar frenetically then freaks out at the din
of a siren screaming but it ain't the cops coming in
just the fire brigade who weave through the jam
before heading for the town centre

14 × 14

                                              there where she
looks at a patch of blue sky listens to the bam-bam
of other daytime sirens plaintive almost that screa-
m and wail that come and go constantly going where
well towards current and future flesh and blood
stiffs or else made of plastic or glass right there
behind the counter of the police station a stud
sits between the urgent case files and the cartridge of
Gitanes blondes (she knows coz last time she got taken in
she was less filthy than she is right now a little love
that evening not out to lunch and dressed winn-
ingly so she decided to play at being the little lost
idiot the result being a night that just cost
her some silly then rather cheeky conversation
followed by rather a long-lasting aperitif that lasted till
early morning (around dawn they even made the decision
to drive her back home in a police car) she will
never forget being shown the undeclared dope hidden
in a safe but tonight no partying why not please
just silence patience fuck-all that period when
minutes becomes hours the goodies the baddies
and the nasty the nice

                              while waiting right here
for example space does what space does
in time as it is perceived by our senses they're

bounded by our physical evolution coz
intuitively so sure of itself just like the eyes
of our anti-heroine only see human-wise
the blank colours of her cell's wall which remain
untouched by the play of unseen violets just
as flashy as the plumage of a bird apparently plain
light brown almost completely seemingly dust

while space anywhere here for example
remains as motionless as a fat fuck
in a fast-food restaurant or an ample
galaxy looking like a distinctly dull star
                              without suck-
ing or screwing coz she simply stinks so much
the door ends up being unlocked the warnings spoken
clearly given and half listened-to the cave of such
sinister copitude is suddenly replaced by open
sky with all its splendid strangely purplish blue
darker than a heavenly bruise so wildly new

Orifices

Orifices of one and the other
are drawn together invisibly potentially
the unnameable becomes perforce nameable
and our mouths whisper sweet nothings
with no apparent interest useless
being so preoccupied with swallowing down our thoughts

by a thousand and one other thoughts
our orifices of one and the other
with no apparent interest useless
but suddenly at random potentially
so full of pretty things
that the unnameable becomes perforce nameable

for it's by speaking of the unnameable
in at least a thousand and one thoughts
decorated with pretty things
that your eyes at last encounter the other
so that finally and at random potentially
the truth that you hear isn't so useless

the truth that you hear isn't so useless
for it's by speaking that the unnameable
takes shape and then potentially
makes concrete all that is unsaid in our thoughts
and that our eyes at last make out the other
and you can sense everything

when you sense this thing
hollowed out or full but the opposite of useless
the one slips into the other
nothing seems unnameable
making concrete all that is unsaid, your thoughts
take form and force potentially

are drawn together powerfully
and our mouths whisper sweet nothings
are so preoccupied with swallowing down our thoughts
hollowed out or full always the opposite of useless
that nothing seems unnameable
and the one enlaces the other

In Bourges

Throwing yourself into the sea of possibility
the water is calm and flat for the moment nothing is happening
all the gulls of potentiality
are on their last legs quiet sleeping hurrying
off like me towards God knows what shit

behind dark glasses the nightmare is over
the bed is hot and humid she has had to leg it
her mad mother with her fucking brother
have finished playing lousy old vampires for fun
have disappeared behind a heavy red cur-
tain or more exactly like chameleons
only visible when the cold makes them move uncer-
tainly and the colour of their skin doesn't change quickly
enough, quick get up bread, butter, coffee
the morning is there like a sea impossible
to navigate it's so totally unruly
and charged with tensions, stupidly inexpressible

and me I take a stroll in Bourges walking slowly
face pallid no longer knowing what to say or who to
there are no messages on my iPhone nothing but spam
the external world no longer seems to

be here but elsewhere the bells sing *I write therefore I am*
but I no longer know what I write or why

in a shop window she reads: *summer is
here rediscover your ideal body shape* it's not really
her problem she is beautiful sweet as a kiss
as they say no that's not her problem at all actually

my movements remain desperately slow and lazy
the old dears the Citröens cheerfully overtake me
I no longer even see them so quickly does the world turn

that's not her problem her problem is that crazy
woman and the nutter in her dreams it's run-
ning to escape mother's axe the fraternal fist
this morning the coffee ices over in its dish
the bread is already stale the butter lightly salt-
ed but without any seafood hake scorpion fish
her chest alone speaks in the void and everywhere
the radio blares with its habitual litan-
y of daily horrors the Tour de France a Berruyère
catches some blasted Mexican
bug you shouldn't eat Tex-Mex don't even try

I ask myself where then I ask myself why
then I ask myself what and when etcetera

then I think fuck it in fact that's what makes me happy

she forgets the radio and its blablabla
everywhere in the world people are dying she
surreptitiously brushes thatch and teeth takes a glance
in the mirror then she's off out the door without locking it
outside the sun is depressing in its brilliance
there's even to cap it all a light breeze fresh and soft
the birdies sing horribly in tune the clouds dizzily
sketch on the azure a grinning snow-
man she feels no rage and no envy
the world turns like milk the roundabout also
with its cargo of horrid kids in the back
in front there's one who's making an awful rack-
et and asking for without realising it a good wallop
and she without realising it what's she a-
sking for to go to Champion and buy a p-
ack of Kronenbourg or to spend the afternoon at the tabac?
no matter in fact it's the price which will dictate

I watch a car then another a couple of vans
they all look alike piss me off there you go mate

the price dictates two super strength cans
and a pack of Marlboro reds then off to the marshes
now beneath her buttocks the grass is soft as lint

a last banger goes by chokes then vanishes
the pigeons croon like a penniless vagrant
like her in fact just like her sitting there kinda
hunched up in her own world with her Stella
in front of the water sticky as gelatine
full of forms that swim about in the gloop
that have no names for her but survive in spite of everything
in this filthy opaque prehistoric soup
the ducks and the ducklings glide about on the surface serenely
as if oiled by the slime while the tourists go
by and go by again in shorts and trainers stupidly
dressed like tourists there's nothing so low
as if a Frenchman when visiting a new shithole or riverbank
suddenly metamorphosed into an American except he still grumbles
for all that she opens the second can her mind a blank

all around me people get pissed and empty their bowels

shut up and listen to the silence for
once it is as dense and thick and stupid as you are
and yes you who are reading this who think you're so clever

there's no longer silence anywhere a lawnmower rev
-s from the other side of the still water the nutter
who manhandles it wears a vest full of
holes his ribs bounce beneath layers of fat

14 × 14

on his face are etched the dregs of all the bottles
emptied since his childhood and then his but-
tocks spilling over his pants form a cleavage more mottled
and protuberant than that of a porn star pumped with silicon

I stop walking why quite simply to stop walking
like a retard like a complete moron
who the whole world tells to walk and who walks without stopping

and you there are you still reading this thing? a moment ago
it was for a laugh you know the poms and their so
visceral craving for a funny gag or
some shit well if it's shit then sorry for bugging
you I stop no longer walking and flee from the water
between the two banks the normal world is sleeping
ears shut tight with two fists to shut out the vocals
while the clouds move gently the sun comes out again
the people who live here the real locals
get on with their diverse means of waiting for the end

she's no longer at the marshes apparently
the silence of the town is more her thing
that's to say the deafening noise which never stops flabbily
never stops filling the surrounding void like lagging
around the cracks of your life every day

she is there in front of you at the counter of the café
trying to work out how to get
as much alcohol as possible for the least outlay in cash

I walk I write I walk and I write without yet
knowing why or how and then there's the catch
so as to avoid getting sunburnt again
I'm obliged to take shelter some part
in a café for example in a confusion
of sounds and smells of scents of drunkenness of shit or of art
lose myself entirely like my Latin in the past
despite the almost incongruous absence of spliffs

you have gone out having refreshed yourself at last
your teeth now as brilliant as the white cliffs
of Dover you find yourself pretty in the glass
a nice bloke looking a bit fun a bit upper-middle class
but in reality seen in the cold light of day
an arsehole of the first order without features of any distinction

at all yes a real bum in a word a phoney
in truth but it's not your fault the generation
of twats before you have a lot to answer for

she stares at her glass perhaps or the lines on her hand her heel
perhaps the fag that she's going to smoke outside perhaps her future

yes but above all so as to feel
free she avoids looking at her neighbour this double
above all you sitting on your stool at the bar

in fact when you think about it you're pathetic with your two-day stubble
but you don't think about this often no for sure for
thinking isn't good for you thinking isn't your thing
when all this is happening or rather not happening
you avoid then doing your head in for nothing
so you avoid almost everything yourself in particular

in front of her Kronenbourg she sits there looking
like a dog beaten by the shit-faced master
that he loves in front of her beer she is like a vast
sea of futures but all utterly impossible
to swallow all leading straight off in front of her towards the past
discovered again and the recurrent and horrible
scene of her nightmares where those who one thinks
one ought to love appear like vampires with eyes
of love of sentiment of warmth that one drinks
like the bowl of milk that one never swallows—she sighs
she goes to smoke her fag in the fresh air

I stop writing think of nothing above all not about her there
in front of me now a cigarette between her lips

she is so beautiful but she doesn't give a shit
for her beauty etcetera is insip-
id and anything romantic absolutely daft
and insincere no chance for you then
the smoke hits her throat with the same force
as the first gulp of air after she was born
she sleeps standing up or almost dreams of straps of truncheons of coarse
carnivorous smiles whose words softly sting
between puffs she stares at whatever for example
the dog shit over there or the indescribable things
strewn about among the butts leaves things not simple
to define the traces of a life of her mother
of herself no doubt of you of me and her brother
without doubt she stares at the glowing end there
of her Marlboro red the papers which are sent flying
about by the wind or for sure the unnatural mother
right in front of her smacking her child tears not even running
from his eyes dry as desiccated sausage skins

I watch you you act as if the world and me were
two completely and utterly different things
we are like two green Martians and then you more
stupid than your shadow and me more stupid than my
arse but it doesn't matter at the end of the day though
she tells herself that nothing matters at the end of the day
her destiny is as banal as that of the woman over there who

crushes or tries to crush the spirit of her little runt
there right in front of her and who affirms himself there right in front
of her in spite of everything who affirms himself under the blows of his
      mother
who refuses to bow down confronted by all this absurdness

I look at the bistro it is bright and clear
like a London smog and its dreary brightness
crushes our eyes tears apart our spirit and we crawl
there the one towards the other in our eyes and in our
spirits while the day breaks apart our dry lips gulp down all
the music of our drinks your eyes pure
as the sea of possibilities there in front of us
the other has gone without leaving a tip
and the barman stares at us and says to us
then what do you want? I want for the moment just to sip
the blue of your eyes your look so slim
in the sea of possible things in which we swim

Listen Out

listen out la parole
est là and we
say ce qu'elle dit

savourons your tongue
stroking ce que ma langue
caresse I mean you

right now parle
dis moi your words
your you quoi

encore tickles a stream
of consciousness un gazouillement
dans l'air this evening

écoutez our words
as we endormons
l'un contre the other

you dream que je rêve
dans ta langue me too
we say tout ça

tu piges where we're at
and tu voles
là où I can follow

I think et je vois
le monde below
and I see le ciel

au dessus and I say
the words de l'air
qui souffle between us

and we wake toi
et moi bercés like that
to life sans mots

No Matter

No matter it begins right there just like that and i-
t will end when the moment comes anyoldhow
probably it won't say very much in the meantime i-
f the pointlessness of real life continues to grow and grow
again ever approaching a world record undreamt of before our
times I mean the void between
your tiny little ears I mean the interstellar
void which chatters on on its own like you sometimes emptying
your umpteenth Kronenbourg for example a good
Bordeaux for example reading books by
people who listen and write like me I guess good
like the whole world sometimes I suppose that's to say
no matter the world in any case trace-
s its path without any apparent intentionality my face
grows flabby yours too and sea levels are
rising apparently allergies spread li-
ke new viruses too and then water
loses its memory in the delirium of the present I
know that we are forgetting everything also that we are practic-
ally made of water that at the end of the day
you and me are like fish out of water so you click
to escape to an elsewhere but it's always here at the end of the day
that you find yourself apparently right

14 × 14

here even the fold in the universe that remains open
to you seems narrower and narrower we laugh at
nothing at all and we carry on
as if for us the world had a meaning yes a meaning one or
the other I mean this way or that way where
you find yourself alone like the last fool yes
and I find myself alone like the first of a new race
of idiots intelligently and stupidly sad and then yes
so alone that their genes will leave no trace
of them for at least the next cycle of creation
waiting perhaps for the consequences of the
reshuffle following the next Big Crunch hey that remin-
ds me we don't have any snacks I need to do a
bit of extra shopping for the kids yes for I'm the
exception to the rule generally
concerning our new race at the
moment reproducing myself like a poor maniac without a legacy
the shop welcomes me like a shop that's to say
with sinister warmth its hand already in my
pocket like a Spanish whore if you know what I mean and then
you ask yourself why Spanish and the answer is
simple why not it makes a change from Brazilians and then
it changes languages also the bone structure the size
of the waist the lips and then hold on where was I then
yes at Carrefour Market to buy some snacks
for the kids so I grab a load of *Big Crun-*

ch then some bananas not too ripe not too black some Yop drinks
and then where was I now yes well
with the Spanish whores with their petite breasts and
their charming little accents as well
as you reach the checkout and then she's not at the end
of the day that awful as cashier-
s go the manager must be her lover or her father
in any case she looks down her nose a-
t you with your not-too-ripe bananas and your Yops and why not a bottle
of rosé as well but organic that's a
bit more upmarket but mademoiselle
couldn't give a flying fart about all that no
matter your natural and flagrant charm
will work next time for sure as with Sandrine no
or whatever she's called the other one who charms
the clients at the Bistro getting them smashed all by herself Amand-
ine that's it you see her there with her fat
ne'er-do-well mates her beautiful almond
eyes or rather nut-brown just like that
sometimes life is absurdly exactly
like that and there's really nothing to say
you almost feel the intelligent design behind it all
another being if you know what I mean who yells and generally
mouths off whether it's the son or the father or the hol-
y spirit no but don't worry it's laughable all that the only
intelligent designer in all that is me bro

if you can call all of that anything other than
ridiculous like a dustpan and brush that goes
straight in there before chucking it into a dustbin that once again
you can no longer open it's so stuffed like you man
with peelings and empty packets of this and that
then you ask yourself suddenly who was the woman
or the man in fact the not-so-smart
designer of these dustbins that no longer open once they're a bit too
full or the ticket machines in the Lille Metro
where on the contrary you struggle to extract your tickets
from the compartment provided like a complete berk
could it be the same person who also created the ticket
punching machines that never actually work
don't trust them these inspectors who come at you with fascist hair-
cuts when you're too stressed to put your finger on the only ticket
not stuck together with a piece of strawberry chewing gum or wor-
se and is it moreover the same person who built
the gare Lille Europe where the four platforms are numbered
from forty-three to forty-six and then their subterranean
location and their various entrances and
then exits make it almost impossible to fin-
d someone who's just got off the train then it-
s complete absence of walls and to cap it
all the fact that one freezes in winter and sweats buckets
in summer is it again the same person
who dreamt up the Bibliothèque Nationale where the books

are suspended in the air exposed to the Parisian
weather and the readers are underground there
are even some rumour-mongers who maintain that the
builders held the plans upside down like here where
they've moved the bloody shelves the bastards where the
biscuits used to be they do it on purpose in fact in the hopes that
in looking for your spuds you'll stumble upon an
irresistible twenty-nine button telly and then without
thinking throw it in with all your Speculoos an-
d what not and then you find yourself there
behind the household cleaning products there's
no logic to it at all but you don't care once you're
outside and the sun strangely illuminates the
huge shiny white deliver-
y van and then all these motors all these motors and the-
ir bodywork which glistens like the eyes of a Spanish whore no
Brazilian rather as it happens with her
false green if not yes blue no
matter contact lenses specially to entice the poor
blokes who queue up in front of her caravan
just as here they queue up to buy their gnats' piss
and then go and drink it in the car park man to man
as well as with the Brazilian who's not exactly bis-
exual in fact but more transvestite and who knows
therefore better than most girls
how to do it if you know what I mean but I'm get-

ting off the point the motors keep coming and going
the tinnies keep getting glugged blokes keep parking get
into arguments the world totters along keeps turning
like a grown-up I really must get back before
the kids expire in front of the telly
for want of a *Big Crunch* and cookies and Speculoos their
stomachs exploding in a Big Bang of gassy
acids as Dora the Explorer keeps on
jumping and skipping while the guinea pigs
squeak in the corner waiting to feast on
carrots and greens and whatnot since like us
they don't manufacture their own vitamin C
I must have said that somewhere or other already
I think but no matter there are loads
of little scientific titbits like that that again and again
merit repeating no and which goad
with their incongruities and then
we move on to something else for example the fact
that someone's wrenched the letter box off the
wall again or has yet again dumped
a load of rubbish of all kinds on the
pavement it was too clean by half well you don't live in this part
of town with its people each more sincerely sincere
than the others well I mean for example it's part-
icularly stupid to ram a billiard queue up the ar-
se of some bloke to be precise

me for not keeping up with the Joneses France
has fallen far lower than your pants the other day when
without thinking you cheated on me just like th-
at like a blind woman without a cane
who walks into a wall and our love story nosedived into th-
e moon of forgotten dreams and unthinkable things
like for example reading from beginning to end these
stupid texts without encountering
diverse and very varied human(s') idiocy(-cies)
right stop those brackets at once it's a bit
too precious besides and the group of
Portuguese who've again drunk too much because shit
as though they no longer know how to use a key as if they've
regressed to the Stone Age they have once more
broken the lock of the front door
to sleep their fists finally clenched tight
on themselves and not in my face for example not up your arse
for example nice eh even if you dig that
apparently but fuck with arse-
holes like that it makes no sense to me no way
each to their own for sure the staircase is half-painted
half-natural like the hand of a Portuguese worker after a long day
the walls have been repainted
in grey and white like the teeth of a Spanish whore and not
to be precise Brazilian certainly not and the
key slips into the lock like into well let's not

14 × 14

talk about that each to their own no in the
end it's not up to me to police your fanta-
sies I don't think so and certainly not vice-versa
I take no responsibility for whatever torments you in the even-
ings when you toss and turn in your big empty
bed while the kids sit in darkness in
front of the telly just like now feeling slightly
ill still waiting for their snacks
which after a long wait finally
turn up in the shape of a pack
of cakes while Dora the Explorer carries on with her monkey
business the world too behind the walls of the
flat even more badly painted than the hands of a
Portuguese at the Bistro below I sit down on the
only chair the kids clamber about all over
bumping into each other in search of a cookie
their eyes all the while glued to the giant screen of the telly

The Blues of a Real Loser

*I used to be a rocker
but from now on
I'm gonna sing the blues
yeah I'm gonna sing the blues
of a real loser*

*for my woman
she's gone and left me
what a shite
what a shite
though you know
as a wage-slave
I was alright
I was really alright*

*now our sex
life is stuffed
what a bummer
what a bummer
though we used to fuck
like rabbits
all through the summer
yeah all through the summer*

(refrain:)
so from now on
I'm gonna sing the blues
I'm gonna sing the blues yeah
I'm gonna sing the blues
of a real loser

then the landlord's liter-
ally kicked me out on the street
with his size 10 boots
with his size 10 boots
though the other
residents
are all prostitutes
you heard me, all prostitutes

then my old man
he's just died
what a stink
what a stink
though you know
everyone told him
to give up the drink
to give up the drink

(refrain)

then my son
turns queer
what was he thinking
what was he thinking
though any bird
was his
for the taking
for the taking

then my daughter
dies from cancer
just my luck
just my luck
though fuck
I love her to bits
I'm just thunderstruck
but just thunderstruck

(refrain ad lib)

14 × 14

At My Place I

This evening nothing this evening love as usual and
so on and then what then what what
life again this evening that's what in the end shunned
she sulks pouts and begs as well enough of that
of life so I change bars fed up with it
of its losers stupid cunts and so on I scarper
she stays stuck there
                                outside still nothing only shit
is being nicked as usual
                                 suddenly without reason her laughter
breaks out on the mirror behind the bar like a
pimple spitting its pus
                                outside not much is being push-
ed as usual it's life real life in the end like a
sheep walking with neither joy nor sadness like a push-
over towards *Eid al-Adha* or to be vacuum-packed for Carrefour

between the old station for hicks and the new one for
Belgian businessmen and so on the short cut
crosses an islet of buddleias galore
grey mallows sinister lilacs birches covered with smut
improvised shithouses kids who're still ador-
able under a layer of filth so thick that it's all the

passers-by see it's on purpose or almost
then the damp rags hanging limply from the
washing-lines between the caravans so still and ghost-
like that the gulls shit endlessly on them then gas
the smell of barbecues of sausages and merguez
with the traces on the soot-dark grass
of fires of older barbecues and then a forgotten fez
just there followed by another then a thigh bone
sucked and emptied thoroughly looking more alone
than a single shark's tooth
        I don't have the slightest no-
tion of what I'm going to do with my life you know I'm
stuck in a kind of how to put it I don't know
you understand in a no man's land between this time
right now which is uncertain and death clearly
arriving at a gallop given the fucking dumb
way I live
   the world turns on I smell nearly
as bad as it does here in the street like a bum
loitering pointlessly
       walk again around the table
and still nothing much to say this evening in which
I swim in a mixture of wine and other reliable
ways to destroy myself for good throw a switch
then shut up while still talking like a fucking local gossip
around the table and I see my dad having a sip

of beer then smoking furtively a cheap cigar on the train
while lying his face off but no one really bother-
ed it was a time when everyone everywhere chain-
smoked without wondering why

                                    yes it's your mother-
s' drooping breast still there just for you in case
you might still need it or something

                                         yes it's
the mystery of life oh yes in which water and a face-
less memory rinses right away your nits
and mesolimbic neurones

                         yes it's about
the evidence now about the existential void
of this universe among others perhaps so you go out
why not you come back home why not you avoid
throwing things away or not as waste may be finally
the aim so don't snuff it too fast I guess at least don't die
this week for example there are just really loads
of things to sort out first yes far too much for instance
my daughter's life

                before the universe implodes
maybe or else stretches itself out for instance
into a more and more diluted soup so full of space
that time will have nothing more to say

                                  you can see
yourself this evening in front of yourself in a place

where you can state your indifference there's the
void in the end no it's not that obvious of course
an indifference about your body for instance
your destiny too that's plain as your face of course
except love still love which shows up from a distance
then flees never mind
                                  the presence of a human body
you can see the flesh still fresh there you sleep deeply
encircled while trying hard not to fart
too much and strangely fleetingly happy

in the supermarket the people who seemed to dart
around like mad while shopping and empty-
ing out their carts now seem to be in slow-mo
taking forever to pick and choose their stuff while
vaguely watching in silence their kids and so
slowly filling out their cheques that you're still in the aisle
thumb-twiddling as they get out their id
cards before looking for a pen so as to sign
and so on and so on yes it's noon already
we're thirsty already and hungry in this line
you can feel it everywhere you can see their gasp-
ing gobs their zigzagged noses you pay you grasp
your stuff then go just anywhere but not where
your feet wander like a girl expelled from a birthday
party here for instance yes exactly there

with nameless streets amid nowhere you stray
or not in fact no not at all you know where you're
going straight ahead for instance you see straight a-
head with your nose starting to (well) nose you snore
on your feet Jesus wake up and pursue a new Eve A
fucking A
                so you go out go out like that dumbly
why not yes just for the sake of going out in fact just
to no longer be there where you were your head firmly
up your arse or even lower down still you get incrust-
ed just about anywhere here for instance where your butt
slides down and comes to a provisional rest but
your senses fall into a provisional sleep while
waiting for what in fact will happen next
that's what the continuation of life by other vile
means flan-like limper than the lips of a sexed-
up beard stuck with spittle heavier than a pat
of butter used in pastries in a bakery store
in Hick Ville yes you go out just like that with your flat
life no more than a vague memory stuck in the manure
of other memories increasingly dissolved in
the generalised entropy of this bar
this evening tonight which is only just beginning
with no apparent end yet caught in the flood of jar-
s of lager and pastis and rosé and white wine
whatever is available right behind the shine

of a chunk of sad zinc among all those
varied tones of brown decking the walls
the shelves the tables the moustaches the clothes
you go out why? do you even know life pulls
you out that's all because this way the time that
will pass anyway will pass in indifferent glee
which is quite intense too yes just like that
like real life existence in other words maybe
in a more concentrated form put on
like an improvised play by a troupe
of blind people on ice
                            now I linger thanks to the sun
the moon gleams beside a flashing street sign a group
of smokers yell in the street and it's as if I were
in the street while in my place wine on the table litterateur
with his balls beneath and all is well
                                      silence at last then
boredom in fact concealed in happiness
while being pleased about feeling fucking dull alone when
the desire to scratch deep down appears yes
which means penetrating quite simply
your fingers into your skin quite precisely there
you can feel it not the place the point precisely
there where it's happening don't you see somewhere
like the desire to tear off your skin in fact wanting
to come why not when you don't have a hard-on

the desire to say what again your life panting
in all its beautiful banality
        amid all this carry-on
the tissues the glasses of water the books barely
looked at you get up and then drag then drag out barely
your body with no apparent reason and then you eat
and drink and so on with no apparent reason
and then you do what the hell why not you make the place neat
hang up your clothes then put the stinking empties on
the street in front of the big filled-up bin dumbly like
everyone else and the street moves and yet doesn't
like every day where the filthy little gippo pik-
ies stick out their hands like every day your constant
usual hypocrisy is a good place to hide who
cares never mind they're all gonna snuff it anyway
just like you too and me as well
        then the impo-
ssible loving hard-on arrives in some mysterious way
all on its own for once like a big tomboy stuck
between your teeth
      I have no reason anymore
          then fuck
at home the great cunt-face gets up and says and so
today I'm cleaning the cupboards so you're helping
to get out the crockery and you do help why you don't know
why in the end I mean what the fuck are you doing

there piling up plates and so on on the kitchen
table with a dumb look on your face like that
even though you can see what life is when
it's real I mean what it means I dunno but not this tat

in the bar over the road they're building a new world
in which everyone respects each other just like
in the good old days and while we're at it the piss-sprinkled
bog overflows
                it doesn't matter not at all on your bike
you useless git
             but a plumber these days
let me tell you will quite simply graze
the skin from your ass and love handles
                                then in the
bar over the road they manage to make all over
a world again and this time it's water hitting the
pastis with its magical touch and then as ever
the sole ice cube melts like a little lonely heart
or something like that
                        yeah in fact and what about
love in all this what do you do with that for start-
ers so with a worldly look and a kind of pout
you're still as uptight sexually and when it comes
down to it as though living alone in the shower or bed
was a life decision a genuine choice for doldrums

as if there was nothing wrong with your head
while a shared bath fuck there's nothing better
in this lousy world of barbies
                           this evening the centre
of the world is your mattress what's happening life
goes on thanks to its own means I mean propagates
itself like a virus talks to itself chats to itself like a wife
turned whore whispers to herself while she waits
on the roadside before before what you can imagine
what never mind you bunch of fuckers all this is
none of your business close your eyes or pick a magazine
showing off desire no I mean the genuine bliss
that makes everyone hard as hell I mean that
a dream body a heavenly screw and then
                                        your
dreams your thoughts whatever calm down or worse shut
up and crawl like a blind baby then what's sure
is that your walls won't open no they're as hard and thick
as a docker's accent
                    how limpid it all is how lymphatic

Alice Slips

Alice slips zips her lip then hides
in a world oh no of your own
yes in a world of your own where things
metamorphose into lexicons
or there you go into banal
graphemachines like a rabbit out of a hole

so coming out of the hole
Alice no longer slips but hides
there she is look in banal
graphemachines recounting a fate like your own
employing the simplest of lexicons
like a world of your own and all her things

there she is Miss Liddell amongst all these things
so coming out of her hole
deploying the simplest of lexicons
where life real life hides
recounting a fête like you and your own
around a table that's utterly banal

around this table that's quite banal
there she is Alice Liddell amongst all her ur-things
the cups the teapot a voice that says oh no
from the bottom of your fate of your hole
where does life real life hide
in a new glossary in your lexicon?

on a new glossary in your lexicon
the extraordinary becomes a banal
cup or familiar cup yes where she hides
Alice the world and all her things
at the bottom of your fate and of your hole
her cups her teapot and that voice that says oh no

in a world of your own
that in like manner metamorphoses lexicons
like a rabbit out of a hole
the extraordinary becomes suddenly banal
just like the world and all its cloud-capped things
the familiar cup the place where you hide

On the Lille Metro

So off we go the train of course but also I guess
this new venture the difference being that the train
"knows" where it's going it'll never stray unless
it derails completely while I'm struggling again
against the current of such a tempting silence
absolutely not knowing where I'm going or
why
      he reads *20 Minutes* daily sense-
lessly for hours made crazy by all those words and more
words which form a puzzle of obscure notions
that tie you to a world of zombies those fool-
s you all reckon with so many commotions
between home and office or home and school
until you die your eyes gaping into emptiness

fake and real fur everywhere spots blotches a mess
of expression wrinkles but with no apparent expression

eyes in a coma once more what's going down
behind all that let's say after about six million
years among which take your pick here an empty frown
not much else apparently apart from chewing
gum and an mp3 player or else a crap awful book

to swallow up time
                         what's she doing?
sitting her knees clamped as though by hook or by crook
a catastrophe was going to hit her right there between
her fat thighs wrapped up in tights she toys with her
little-girl earrings then redoes her plaits clean-
s her eyes makes them up again staring emptily cunt drier
than my mouth agape as it is God knows why
                                                    to-
night no one speaks anymore reads anymore except him his two
earpieces God knows why stuck over his head of greasy hair

at Mons Sart (which means what in fact?) they
snooze off even more deeply between a *Marie Claire*
and some crap classic R&B who gives a fuck in fact hey
what does it all really matter when all is said and done

I'm sitting next to a guy who should be made
to pay for two seats and like practically everyone
wash his clothes sometimes
                             a lettered maid
is reading *Pride and Prejudice* in English in front of me
I follow the emotions on her face guess-
ing the passage she's reached
                             look see
another case creating a void around the mess

this one's in like a safety perimeter surround-
ing a Seveso factory then me like the profound
hypocrite I am I draw away as well the better to hear
the guy yelling out further on in the carriage about the
fact of having been born and above all not just anywhere
but in France monsieur yes in France madame blather-
ing on before getting off at Place de la République Beaux
Arts as it's called these days and the so-called "Mediation"
agents stop pretending to talk about footy and so
on among themselves without the slightest shame or hesitation
staring at the opposite end of the carriage before
finally turning around to follow the troublemaker's back
which is now moving away just as endless bore-
dom divorces the body from its victim's soul in a total lack
of understanding why
                           now it's more me being stared at
just like I've been staring at them it's as if when sat
in the metro your face has not at all been
made really to be looked at despite
all those millions of years made up of a gene
stream of brows and noses and chins all looking shite
on an equal footing
                  a change of sides
but not really a change of perspectives or face-
s remain it's dark outside dark in the eyes
of my co-travellers all going I guess someplace

extremely precise as opposed to me now
wandering with no other aim than to fill in this page
without really thinking about what's awaiting me or how
I'll survive I guess meanwhile taking an age
about it Transpole is taking me to Roubaix float-
ing on a dream then back to Fives with my throat
dry my body senseless which puts itself on the way
there into a dark corner of the train once more
between the fire extinctor and a black lady
whose ample ass (and the rest of her too) for-
ces me to adopt a weird leaning posture at
the same time being almost twisted into a spiral
while under me my backpack and legs are bent at
an extremely acute and arthritic angle
then one and two elbow blows to my chest while the train's
jogging is giving me a vaguely odd underground
feeling of being seasick I shift a little she then aims
for my liver already sensitive enough without her pound-
ing what to do? stop writing? try to change my seat?
stand up? but stubborn as the smell of my feet
I stay sat there pen in hand always in the hope
of arriving somewhere I'd like to stay a bit
longer but of course without giving any rope
at all not an inch to love or eternit-
y or other similar trifles in the tweet-
like transgenerational flow of illusions which can be

optical or psychic who cares in the end the street
summons me then like you then it rejects me
but fuck let's talk about something else nearly
at Lomme the little beggar boy who's been pound-
ing out unwearingly his automatic refrain finally
reaches us and wow something really rare around
here he manages to get a few coins from a young uptight
miss with a big gold-studded handbag and fishnet tight-
s while the grannie opposite with a wrinkled ball-like
head stays cold as marble and my good self as well
shit think what you want I never give to kids
                                              on your bike
Lille and now Lambersart (a town as swell
as a London suburb with its cloned houses/
gardens) runs above our heads I'd rather snuff
it than live there or even get off at this
station for a coffee so I turn back enough is enough
I'm not tempted by IKEA or the bar on the main drag
(HQ of the Club of Hunters of Lomme (hear
"man" weird name innit)) here the rag-
boys don't beg (see explanation above) it's clear
gippos aren't as daft as all that
                                  the train slowly
fills up but now in a kind of "no man's time" nei-
ther this nor that between the morning rush hour
and lunch peopled by North Africans everywhere

as idle as all these grannies except just look at our
pale egghead with short but tied-up filthy hair
who is reading *Science et Vie* while tapping
his chin with a doubtful look on his face
then the approach both of Lille and napping
after lunch put a collective crowd in place
with uniform youths all missing out on their
rebellion as a herd of beasts following a shove
this way a yell that way all copied from neat hair-
ed talking heads
                       then with the moon above
almost swamped out by the lighting of the train
Lille Sud arises in its soulless rain-
seeped glory before vanishing just as quickly
as the metro dives back again into the abyss
of the Porte des Postes
                              it's time to go home to see
if chips are on the menu while the train is
filling up with massive butts and thighs prop-
ping up chubby arms and hands carrying equally
huge bags marked C&A and H&M or shop-
s boasting even more obscurely
allusive abbreviations if this goes on
we'll soon have to do like the Yanks who
having bought from our wonderful Alstom
a 100% automatised driverless metro

for Florida then had to cut down the maximal
number of passengers given their weight and the overall
quantity of flesh and so on being run about during
each journey
              the chill of the night arrives in short blast-
s when the doors open before the blaring
of the closing signal and then off we go at last
for another game of ping-pong the sudden dit-
ching of fleshy warmth is chilling after all
and the stations go by one by one Bourg then Mitt-
erie and still in this dim dark night fuck all
that breaks this monotony until Canteleu
where a guy about my age gets on carrying
a bag that stinks of chips which are going cold the
fat they swim in getting gooey this has been going
on for six no seven stations now phew at number eight
he finally gets off his chips in a state
which is unimaginable (anyway it's up to you
to try if the idea appeals to you it don't to me bud)
while right in front of me are now sitting two cu-
ties each with a lughole occupied by an earbud
very cute but so young shit far too young for you
you old fucker
              can the metro be considered maybe
like just about any other place old or new
in other words as something that we

can take with us wholly anywhere exactly
like an ill-digested madeleine giving you
repeaters anytime for instance like the moon you see
sparkling on the snow which just came down as you
were thinking about what nothing more than
usual except for an imaginary metro man-
-oeuvring crazily towards a destination so
forgettable like the real world in which snow
melts as fast as a quiche in the micro-
wave you've just bought now shedding a red glow
while flashing pointlessly on the worktop
of your dreams
                      can we then consider that the fat
fucker there in front of you grumbling yawning non-stop
on his way home this evening symbolises just that
a fat fucker grumbling yawning on his way
back to wifey this evening or else that the in-
evitable bum who stinks like high hell in a way
that's just as inevitable symbolises in
his own way the clear advantage of chasing away
those fucking yoofs playing tedious tunes every which way
even more dumbly than their dress sense getting right
in my lugholes while he also makes flee all those mums
with their filthy buggies with piglets with night-
marish comforters creating about the same effect as bums
(no piglets can't be the appropriate word

we've slumped back into a basic xenophobia
so screw it let's get off go for a not yet slurred
drink or two at Karim's for redemption ra-
ther than continuing rolling off this kind
of crap phew yes we're almost at metro Fives
it's coming up before my eyes find-
ing their feet so to speak as people pour in like every eve-
ning here's my personal terminus my spot
for some time now) so shall I buy more bread or not?

Filthy Time

time is dead
like you dad
like you mum
time is dead

time is dead
like us
like you beneath me
both of us spent

then suddenly like time
there we are once more
ticking like time
which begins to quicken

no it doesn't quicken time
it's us
who pass through time
like ghosts

ghosts who spend time
stupidly
not knowing what else to do
with time

time weighs
us down
so what should we do with time
but kill it?

I Thought Everywhere

I thought for example scratching my ball-
s about a sincere poem that talked about you b-
ut no
      next I thought about nothing really nothing at all
it was the king-sized void in my empty king-sized b-
ed the neurones apparently dead the sy-
napses minced then it was morning all of a sudden
like a rock

      next hiding under my duvet I
thought about you yes you and us who have sudden-
ly become invisible at least in the mean
eyes of the public at large and certainly to the small bunch of
people who read me looking for a good sex scene
and there you are damn all this time but what a bunch of

next I thought about what follows all of that shit
what follows the life of my body and it-
s continuation on earth by other means for example
in a bistro
      and then next I
thought about my situation from a financial angle
then I stopped almost immediately I

was fucking freaked out
                          next I thought
about the presidential elections and which can-
didate I would vote for
                          and then subsequently I thought
that I'm English and so actually I can'-
t vote here even though I pay taxes and I've given four stout
and completely white children to this sweet secular nation

and then I thought about tomorrow
                                    then I thought about
nothing apparently saying to myself that the iron-
y of all that is that France at one point in history
was a supporter of the Yankee revolution which screa-
med *no taxation without representation*

and then I thought that's all I thought in a dead
sort of neuronal no man's land without taxation

and then I thought I thought that's all
                                  the runes said
what tell me again just useless things when all's said and done
tragic things nothing of any impor-
tance I mean to say come down to earth when all's said and done
we can still have an argument
                                    and then I thought that the door

in front of me is as ugly and badly painted as you
my ex-lover my I dunno actually
                           and then I
thought once more yes about the elections me who
doesn't vote as you know because clearly I'-
m English for example or Arab no matter
sweet France will clearly be stronger
if we don't vote we who don't deserve to
have French citizenship and then

I thought about this whole mass of people even blondes who
aren't French whether they deserve to be or not

                                                            then

I thought about something else so as not to stress my-
self out with existential question-
s for example is there any rosé left in my
fridge? no I don't think so it's all drunk and then
shit
    I thought I'd better go to Carrefour
Market or even to make a change the Petit Casino
in front of the Town Hall to buy some or-
ganic rosé why not then some uneco-
logical fizzy water and vod-
ka while I'm at it while the world
is heading who knows where
                                      then I thought it's crazy

how ridiculously some lover-
s behave
                then I thought that in fact the family
is worse still these people get on your tits hanging ar-
ound whichever way you look like the fucking police
they look straight through you in fact it's like
you didn't even exist like a piece
of shit on the carpet of a show house like
some free verse hidden under your duvet lonely as a
bum without a dog you find yourself in the boule-
vard of lost desires carrying on your back a
for God's sake completely not cool
inheritance made up of nightmares of lies of inanities
of silences of false smiles of mythologies
of toasts made to nobody etcetera yes ri-
ght you find yourself there like the last moron
still asking yourself stupid questions but li-
fe is elsewhere you know you feel like a dwarf on
the shoulders of other dwarves all looking in
the wrong direction
                        next I thought
about life on other planets without God or sin
or the devil but with other myths space-thought
among them the belief that people are not
people but the shadows of a divine being
who doesn't exist either or that all the souls and whatnot

14 × 14

above all your own fold themselves up into the teen-
iest little crevices of a space made of seven-
teen dimensions becoming thereby invisibly etern-
al or else that everybody is forbidden to l-
ove one another and above all that you mustn't love your
parents who are after all your number one enemy on a l-
ist of one hundred and eleven containing all your
friends and neighbours the whole crew
and then the idea that the imaginary is more powerful than
logic I mean like with some bizarre sociologists who
maintain that mathematicians are in
fact culturally biased
                          and then I thought about
you yes I can't stop myself apparently I'-
ll have to get used to it for the time being unt-
il it wears off a bit or completely and I
can start life all over again
                          then I thought that
thinking like that does no good at all and that
I'd be better off getting a lobotomy
                          an-
d then I thought that even if it's been prove-
d that neutrinos travel no faster than
photons and therefore light that doesn't prove
that the universe isn't jam-packed with other things which
travel so much faster than light that you can't even

detect them or even tell where they are which
would explain all the so-called dark matter which in
fact is blindingly luminous which apparently
is missing from the balance sheet of this world
            and then I
thought that exactly like whisky
you exhaust me at the same time you excite me li-
ke vodka too I suppose
        then I thought that the recently converted
who stupidly believe that the good
Lord has chosen them and not me or you for ex-
ample are fundamentally arrogant just like those shit-
hot sporting stars who announce publicly that they're ex-
ceptional thanks to God too
        and then shit
I thought that to say you're proud of being Fren-
ch is just as stupid as saying you're proud
to have ten fingers for example or two testicles/ovaries it all depen-
ds and that now in addition people want you to be proud
of your region wherever you happen to be from but
frankly you must be out of your mind whether you
buy this or whether you don't to think that
you might have some particular merit because you
happen to be born in one place rather than
another like in the north for example rather than

14 × 14

the dear non-existence of God in Nice
                                          and th-
en I thought about deep-sea fish and their strange head-
s that pull a face even better than you do but th-
at are yes just as exotic when all's said
and done as you but far less ugly on the other
hand
        and then I thought about the exobiologist-
s who try to determine whether or not other
possible beings pollute their atmosphere just
as stupidly as we do on their exoplanet
which still exists perhaps given the speed of light
or maybe it doesn't
                        and then I thought
again about you and your thighs your tight
arse etcetera right think of something else why
not think instead yes about the Bose hi-fi
that you dream about no not that it's too much
the new iPhone no not that either it's a crying shame
how much the world is stuffed with such
irresistible physical and abstract goods so flam-
ing sexy that even an exoplanetary microbe would fl-
ip its lid (and above all for your thighs (in
fact while I'm thinking about it what's the name of that fl-
ipping Irish saga where a queen offers herself thighs and all in
exchange for a peace treaty shit

The Táin I think but no matter actually the image alone is en-
ough to how shall I put it yes make it
stick in the mind))
                        there you are an-
d then I thought about depression and its infin-
ite capacity to be shite as well as irration-
ally obstinate in its behaviour like you
say of a mule while being at the same time the
elephant in the room right there as you
talk about what about us for example for we
breed like rabbits
                        then I thought how no-
one's ever explained how you can tell wh-
en someone's staring at your back or your neck even though
you can't see them it's odd is it because of that wh-
ite or black rather matter which holds the
universe in equilibrium and somehow transport-
s invisible particles from one body to another
I think and even start to worry about why I've thought
about so many stupid things trying to
yes think about nothing again so as to
die all the same you're not as dumb as all that nor as quick
either and actually it could be worse
you're not in a retirement home for example where your dick
is masturbated by an open-minded nurse
you get back to sleep at last perhaps it was a m-

ale nurse but you're so ill you don't care really

then I thought at once of something else M-
onday morning for example after a completely
depressing Sunday yes almost as de-
pressing as the PMU café in which
I write these verses even more rickety than me

then I thought that decidedly it was time to
stop thinking and instead and instead what to
bet on a horse like the other people here for
example have another rosé like the other
people for example stroke a mutt uglier than me for
example among other things you wonder
why people spend so much time and shit
money on the horses and on cheap
rosé when if you think about it
they could spend it fucking between glasses of champ-
agne and especially when you see
trotting during which the daft aim is to make
your horse go slowly you'd be better of watchi-
ng the paralympics expecting a record break-
ing pole vault from someone in a wheelchair
                                                        then I thought
that I've thought too much yes no question I ought

[2]*Forget It Never Mind (I)*

forget when I tell you to get lost
forget when I tell you I love you
the moment's not there this evening
the moment escapes us tonight
the room is reduced to us
the room opens to all

the room opens to who knows
forget when I tell you I'm going out to buy cigarettes see you later
the room is reduced to this music
forget when I tell you that it'll be fine tomorrow all the same
the moment is still there
the moment goes on and on

reason goes on and on
the house opens to who knows
reason is still there
laugh when I tell you I'm going to buy cigarettes see you later
laugh when I tell you that it'll be fine tomorrow all the same
the house is reduced to this music

---

[2] To lie through my teeth

the house casts its shadows
reason also
laugh when I finally cry
the house is sufficiently sturdy
laugh when the sky shits snakes
reason stands up in the darkness

life stands up in the darkness
the void casts its shadows
fantasise when the sky shits snakes
the void also
life is sufficiently robust
fantasise when I finally cry

fantasise when I tell you I love you
life escapes us tonight
life's not there this evening
the void opens to all
the void is reduced to us
fantasise when I tell you to get lost

At My Place II

This morning still nothing I get up shite
no choice apparently to piss and then
drink some more water to start with white
coffee and hey a cognac for instance
                                            when
the sun rises again like a yellow hole it lingers stu-
bbornly in front of me and my computer and my empty
glass looking for a target as in a marketing stu-
dy finding out whether for over fifty-
year-olds wrinkles are totally unbearable or else
the real reasons for the difference between
the so-called swallowers who are repulse-
d by chewing gum out of principle but are keen
on sucking sweets just like me and then the
non-swallowers who do the opposite as you can see
my dietary habits are largely useless
given that I'm definitely heterosexual
I'm afraid having tried out the odd caress
with an old mate and didn't like it all
no not one little bit but maybe he
just wasn't the right one you might point out
that's possible but still I'm really
not starting over I'm afraid even though about

14 × 14

all the girls I know well went through a lezzer
period during their youth given that
there's nothing clumsier than a young geezer

the sun ends up coming through the shutter slat
by slat like a handicapped burglar slink-
ing a first leg over the jamb one foot in the sink
without even knowing what he can or wants to
steal as thick as the guys who broke in-
to my old place in Paris and for fuck's sake nicked two
posters stuck on the wall of Matisse painting-
s I mean what stupid cunts
                                      back around the table
and still nothing happens the walls still need a coat
the dishes to be done but my life becomes stable
again oddly enough I'd better shut up than gloat
I think better go back to bed and sleep
                                                  meanwhile
the sun insists about getting into my place
like a girl you no longer love trying out every guile
on your limp body no name no names nor paint a face
of course there'd be no point
                                meanwhile
you get up and look at yourself in the mirror a smile-
less face is sending you the same message as your

brain
        meanwhile never mind time passes just as though
it had nothing else to do with its own time the whore-
sun changes places and wakes up the neighbours the low
and primary woman apparently hooked on hairy
chests each to their own quite clearly I mean if I were
as gay as Gordons (though Bombay Sapphire is really
gayer by far) I honestly reckon I'd prefer
smooth guys like me I mean isn't that one
of the mysteries of sexuality that is to say
the charm of this person or that depending on
the total difference or else the display
of an almost identical physical identity of bodies
(or better why not among missed memories
there's one in particular when two girls
(one pretty as hell the other so-so (but each to
their own after all (for me the brunette)) with curls
and all clearly wanted to screw me to-
gether and I said no (later I wondered whether
it was a kind of highly evolved self-protection
instinct against Aids among other
things just like the supposed protection
when raped (I mean really) that women
have against getting pregnant (according to
the Republican party) but I no longer care when
stuck as I am inside all these brackets I'm lost (you

too I imagine)))))
                       and then the sun
then the sun then the sun then the sun
stays there stays there stays there stays there stays there
like a cunt like a cunt like a cunt who invites himself
to your place without a bottle of plonk and stays there
sitting like a dickhead gormless in front of a shelf
of porno films
                  how odd how odd to be hit on
like hell by a geezer with a Lillois working-class look
who gazes into your eyes then plays footsie upon
which he actually suggests coming up to my place the hook
being to watch a footy match well it makes a change
from etchings I suppose I suppose a case
of shifting representations innit a change
of tone in this neighbourhood like the pretty face
of that bird who works the bars (how much per
night I have no idea not that dear I reckon from her
charming conversation I was listening
into (yes honestly listened into really only
you know I never lie about this kind of thing
or practically) I was where yes there lonely
like a Normandy oyster or another from the west
coast of the USA for instance
                              the moon
looks at itself in a mirror of water then does its best

panting like an old computer on a porn site spoon-
ing with you and your thigh while it's at it
and why not going further and higher oh yes
there exactly there oh yes and more that's it
sleep now sorry I was a bit too quick but your caress
is just so fucking right so fucking spot on
                                              the moon
looks at itself again like you in an arctic mirror like a goon
like the dumbest cunt imaginable while the sun
is starting to heat its buttocks so an eclipse can begin

you get up again without any given reason
because that's what we do in this world inn-
it not even for a need to pee for once really not
no coz you have to drink as well so as to be able
to piss later on and so on outside the world's grot
goes on so blankly so charmingly that you're incapable
or nearly of noticing it so what to do then
back to bed or go on make some tea for instance or coffee
why not hot chocolate yuk definitely not so then
sliced buttered bread cornflakes whatever the
required things to fill your gut before attacking life
in all its quite literal trouble and strife
if you see of course what I mean
                                         what about love
in all of this you might ask and certainly

14 × 14

will of course coz it's a story you'll never get enough of
which you spill your guts about quite clearly
adore the cunt that I am and it will all go
just like our inexistent God wanted it to

then meanwhile the sun heats itself up so
much it fries Australian heads which must burn too
in the streets nowadays well anyway when
they're not out surfing or playing cricket
for instance
               so let's face up to this again
to this shithole so I surf to see who's winning the cricket
and this evening it's definitely no longer England not
at all it's all falling apart with this team which is clearly not
dissimilar to the French footers after the world cup
oh yes you can spot the real cunts quite clearly
when they succeed
                     at home time to sup
some soup with God knows what in it lardy
shite galore yum thanks my darling lady
love
      tonight's stars twink at each other from afar like
two teenagers in a nightclub clutchingly
in four imaginary arms caught in the strik-
ing draw of their own deep gravity right on their own
meanwhile we continue don't we we go on

you see like oddly enough you're known
to me as me to you but anyway it goes ever on
so here you are with your fucking love
which pisses you off like God fucking above
as nostalgic as Ulysses up to his usual shit

red giants in tales for kids told by
extremely qualified astrofissicians lit-
erally do and make what they know so well i.
e. other splendid red giants before they
become blue then white dwarfs I think while
aging more badly than you at the moment hey
I know no more about astronomy than all you style-
less freaks who cares
                    who cares
                                  who cares our sun
continues to do its stuff and you too right
there in front of your guts your facebook fun
filtering your life slowly like a soup of you slight-
ly in it too much water not enough meat or anything
else giving it a taste of something
like mealy lard
                    meanwhile a giant or dwarf
goes about its business as business generally goes on
while the supernovas strut their stuff
                                    then morph

14 × 14

away wisdom fucks off like an eighteen-year-old coward done
down to looking at himself suddenly physically
in the ice in the fridge as well as the vodka
of his memories
                 who cares
                             the ice/water frankly
never lies just like you don't of course ah
no I shake my head like the stupidest git
or the brightest one maybe who cares really
I'm not translating this bit really but making it
up given that the French doesn't go smoothly
into English at all so fuck it who cares wench
or geezer if you're reading this it means you can't read French

the sun goes about its own business too
                                         the
moon as well
               who cares how to count this time
that passes seemingly on its own just like tha-
t seemingly fuck knows how like one plus one don't rhyme
with two no more than with a tiny Renault or like the truck
that crushed your kid
                         who cares you set
off again once you've taken it on board you fuck-
ing obviously need to get on with it coz life is get-
ting its boots on to screw you up yes you right there

this evening in front of your computer and your belly
which feels so alone if only it could piss itself (where?)
right there
                who cares
                              and the sun finally
wakes you up anyway making you walk to
a fridge of things ranging from rancid butter to
limp veggies but above some rosé
dripping its condensation like your forehead its
taste now runs down into your mouth which is gapey
like a river pissing itself into the sea tits
forgotten you just swallow its salt so right
so lapped up like a green recycling like
I don't know what comes next a porn site
for instance writing something because crike-
y (crap English) I need to finish this pile of crap
who cares go to the supermarket again
where everyone is lined up like Jap-
s recently arrived so love seems then
impossible between two glances between us
with awkward shopping bags sitting on the bus

But Now

but now I drink but now
at home I drink at home
all alone I drink all alone
this night I drink this night
and so I drink and so
just anything I drink just anything

and you you eat and you
all alone you eat all alone
the evening you eat the evening
at home you eat at home
the silence you eat the silence
still there you eat still there

you know they say you know
us alone they say us alone
you die they say you die
all alone they say all alone
you dream they say you dream
nothing else they say nothing else

you see they say you see
just anything they say just anything
the meaning they say the meaning
of life they say of life
your thoughts they say your thoughts
you burn they say you burn

with me you see with me
this evening you see this evening
my hands you see my hands
on you you see on you
my mouth you see my mouth
all over you see all over

your fingers I smell your fingers
on me I smell on me
you alone I smell you alone
at night I smell at night
the silence I smell the silence
of you I smell of you

I Thought Again

And then I thought again again and again
of you of me of all of you of us everybody e-
qual as they say dragged down to the bottom yes again
again and again
                      and afterwards I thought more precisely
of you in relation to me in relation exactly
to the force that determines whether one wants it or
not each human or not relation habitually
or fleetingly passionate and ultimately substanceless more
runny than the flan in the canteen harder than e-
quations to the fifth degree
                                  then I thought that
you there me there well you and me we-
're like all the little blokes and like pract-
ically all the little chickies yes that's to say equal to
two equations divided by zero like the two
square roots of just about any
number the two of us for example you posit-
ive me negative or the opposite carrie-
d away by the irrational in any case drift-
ing towards the infinite like neut-
rinos slower than light and a lot higher

than our respective backsides
                                  and then I thought
about the fact that being two and irrational is er
more beautiful than being alone me always sadly eq-
ual to myself and you in the rectangular square of i-
maginary girls
                        and then I thought about what let's speak
of Georges Perec and how the fact of having translated hi-
m changed my life just like the fact of going out
to have a drink one evening just to be out and about
was absolutely necessary this drink at this time and not elsewhere
and then you were there and you are still there
                                                                                then
I thought again about Perec his apparently care-
less way (yes apparently I say it again)
of laughing and joking in the face of the enormit-
y of life of his own life of years when you think
about it no when you wake up and grab it
like a clammy and virtually unknown pink
hand traversing a panic so hot and mute
                                                         then I
thought about love but all of a sudden minus my
love for you you see and not about so-called li-
fe but about words and about their letters making an infinitely
flexible material in his so skilful
hands that nonchalantly constructed verbal

14 × 14

fortresses so as to conceal th-
e slow suicide of cigarettes and alcohol
and then I thought quite stupidly th-
at it's you Georges Perec who is quite ridiculousl-
y the dead person that I would choose to meet if
I passed some hairbrained recruitment test s-
o as to awkwardly and pointlessly qualif-
y to take part in a study it's hard to be s-
pecific on shaving foam for ex-
ample the kind of question that one asks to find out if you can
manage to just about align one lex-
icographically rich word after another but I'm a northern-
er and then to translate marketing
on the hop like Perec would be following
my instinct would at the time when he wrote *Thing-
s* that's to say immersed in the world to find out why we
sell our souls for a sofa more pin-
k than your right buttock is soft and thicker than the ephemerality
of love
        then I asked myself why
this question has become so much more depressing
than at the time I mean now why
does it reach wham right onto your being
into your corporeal bones do you see what I mean no yes
right there do you see like that you see like hell
yes the world which what which well interpellates yes

you and your frustrations with your messed-up desires as well
like a recruit fleeing the war in Algeria for
example like a worthless student who parodies or
mocks the existence of a worthless student li-
ke a letter which crumbles like a world that takes f-
orm precisely there in front of the blind man illuminated by
the moon a non-existent address
                                     then f-
rustrated little by little then more and more I go blindly by
towards what towards you for example
I no longer know in reality why my
head leads me like that then little by little
you couldn't give jack shit anymore and a bl-
onde looks at herself in the mirror and finds herself more and more little
by little ugly and sad and well weird like a bl-
ue bruise that turns pink and yellow and mauve just as two little
nothings end up looking like two bollocks
                                              I
love you it's a sort of I dunno little by
little lie to oneself a bit less for example ball
out *gnothi seauton* for a bit

more I think that little by little entropy overtakes all
the world rambles like us towards a state where it
sucks the blood of atoms like a universal Social Security
Collection Agency with a specialised Worker-

's Social Security behind each translator jack of all trades every
plumber too and each shit decorator
too while I'm at it
                              then I thought that bit by bit
our love unties itself like the laces of
your pumps and the sleeve of your jumper but not the shit
leather of my black jacket
                              and then I thought of
how to think bit by bit less and less would be
a liberation as enormous as had be-
en the first sight of Paris in the somewhat hypocritical view
of quite a few of its citizen-
s and those silenced and actually shedding a few
tears faced with the beauty of it all
                              then
I thought of who of what well of the very "big" in all senses of the
word Jacques Roubaud and the fact simply
that I lost it hardly dared to speak to him the
day we caught sight of each other for the very
first time it was after a seminar held by the Asso-
ciation Georges Perec at Jussieu where he
read a paper called The Po-
lish Model I can even remember the
exact date for unless I'm completely mistaken
the fascicule of the B.O. had just been published en-
titled *L'e muet* by him

and Jacques Jouet and we were passing it from hand
to hand to take a look at it and I felt so dim
and insignificant in relation to all that and
above all because of him but not yet because of Jacques Jouet
who I'd barely even had a chat
with I almost wanted to do a runner straight away
and it was only many years yes many years later that
now a member of this strange workshop I
found out that it was actually Roubaud for
me the "biggest" in all senses of the word poet in the ni-
ght of our agony in bed or elsewhere in the darkness or
not it doesn't matter who had a vision of poetry
that in the end I shared shared truly
it was Roubaud in short who who solicited my non-
candidature to Oulipo shit the sheer joy
unbelievable
              and then I thought about the *Chanson
de Roland* and its rhymes and its rhymes which deploy
their sense and their music like a beautiful stutterer announc-
ing her love
              and then I thought about love
or rather its absence its inexistence
its nullity its death gone forev-
er like a letter to Italy or a Corsican
civil servant at the photocopier or like

reason/politeness in the case of an old fart
                                              an-
d then I thought about the dark energy which rises out of nowhere like
all the things you no longer think about for ex-
ample the fact that you haven't had sex
without paying for it like normal consensual and un-
protected sex for a month of Sunday-
s or for a fuck of a long time if not exactly a month of Sun-
days in the space where you're trapped as ridiculously
as your conscience grabs your body as ridiculously
as your snatch holds my cock as ridiculously
as love or even you made me quite ridiculously
feel like what like that I was simply
there quite simply there and not elsewhere the-
re between you
                        and then I thought of the good things I know
about facebook for there are some all the same like the
almost complete disappearance of slide show-
s among so-called friends or parents awkwardly
showing off moments of idiotic intimacy
or some clichéd landscape which would wipe the smile
off your face more rapidly than an in-depth study of the
Mid-West mile by fucking mile
or even scenes of a shared moment of joy th-
at you'd be hard-pressed to understand
that would leave me completely in the dark

you too to boot and worse still those bland
people who pass round their Polaroids while you're park-
ed on the sofa in front of a
glass of undrinkable white wine and a telly
blabbering on in the background that's now showing a
magical sketch among many others by Monty
Python with family photograph-
s passed around for a laugh
along a sofa twinkling in its brown
ugliness yes family photos which their victim tears up one a-
fter another before throwing them down
on the floor that's it the good thing you can say a-
bout social media which obliterates the horror
of looking at other people's photos unless you're a
real masochist
      and then I thought er
really about nothing then you come in hey it's like a
gift one of the most precious evolutionarily
speaking that's to say something quasi-
papal in a totally non-religious sense if you even temporarily
see what I mean and then and then for a moment li-
fe and the world continue to turn round
aimlessly as if nothing had happened
it almost makes you want to what want
to throw up yes
      and then I started to think again

14 × 14

dumbly like the last cretin or the last forgotten cunt
and what does that do for me in the en-
d not much truth to tell same as everyone else more or less
you could say
                     and then I thought completely stupidly that
the best thing that had happened to poetry or just about the bes-
t of all was quite simply and quite ridiculously that
it no longer exists that it's impossible
or something of the sort
                             and then I thought what's everyone got
against gay marriage it's not possible
there aren't that many closet paedophiles as all that not
even here living quietly on their own it's a joke
                                        and then
I thought of you and the last time when . . .

The Insect Contemplating

The insect contemplating prehistory etc.
while we contemplate the sum
of an entire world train-
ing to write made-to-measure texts before it's out
into the night
which crosses all this, what do you say?

who crosses over this place, what do you say?
the man in the street etc.
nothing but a comma in this night
while we calculate the sum
of immeasurable cries before it's out
from the train

in this train
in motion, the fat controller might say
the time has come get out
the man in the street etc.
we are in sum
only a comma in the night

while across England, this night
crosses the train
—us in sum—
in motion and the arsehole controller will say
—rail bellow argue cry etc.—
the hour is here please get out

but how can we get out?
while across England the night
rails bellows argues cries etc.
turning over the train
and then quickly it says
we're crushed and then make a sum

thrown out of the carriage in sum
but how the hell can we get out?
Right down there? So say
what it's all about this night
of an entire world train-
ing itself to contemplate the insect contemplating prehistory etc.

On the Train

It doesn't matter it really doesn't matter finally
that I didn't get the window seat I
asked for my phone starts to ring annoyingly
I can't bear chatting like that baring my
soul in front of the whole bloody crew
and then there's this horrible kid who's balling out
you can't hear yourself think sometimes you
start to wonder and above all above all about
that in fact I mean why the hell did I go through the most
painful operation to get my hearing
back when in actual fact being deaf as a post
has so many obvious advantages at times like being
thick for example sometimes comes in handy or
like being ugly can sometimes make you look cool or
being made in China can help sell noodles

                                          the raindrop-
s trickle quietly down the windows changing their direction
depending on the speed of the train while drop by drop
I swallow what life throws at me vodka the overwhelming sensation
of being completely and utterly alone
with the subjacent question as to whether or not
it's better to live like this for all concern-

ed or whether rather I would be just as well or badly or not
off tied to the stake that you offer me meanwhile the
liquid starts to dry out on the windows an-
d in my stomach and I see that even the SNCF make use of a-
naphora to underline the seriousness of its commitmen-
t to eliminating every form of discomfort so you have
no chewing gum on the floor please and then you have
no use of your mobile phone please and then you have
no I can't remember please who cares but you have
no something or other please in any case then out of
the window you see stranger and stranger kinds of
buildings and stuff like from an abandoned mini
theme park a rusting car parked in a ditch then cara-
van after caravan and then one depressi-
ng backwater after another depressing ba-
ckwater and you start to wonder why the train
always goes through the most desolate of places the-
n the obvious answer hits you straight away it's down
to local elections and the stupidity of the
electorate but still there's no law against annoying
kids and their parents (equally annoying)
who pretend to be bothered by the fact they're pissing
off a whole carriage nor against the black lady opposite
who's asking her mobile how come her fucking
ex has found out her new address and how is it
that the goddess who's just got off the train

didn't leave hers it almost makes you regret the dis-
appearance of smoking carriages which stank to high heaven
for sure but which were full of beautiful smokers with no dis-
gusting children in fact yes there should be a law for-
bidding young parents from travelling
unless they've knocked out their kids fir-
st either physically or chemically it doesn't matter and forbidding
them from going about as if they've just won the lottery
when in actual fact they had a bad fuck then lai-
d the latest of their four brats

                              another journey
new friends and ridiculous new fur collar-
s manufactured from real animals or else from really
sad and fluffily disgustingly synthetic fur
made in China as well by former
Tibetan monks and other prisoners of an
undeclared and bitter civil or rather
uncivil war

                   and then in my headphones the songs of Anne
Sylvestre which haven't lost any of their magic create the nec-
essary buffer between myself and the world so
that these writings on my iPad creep forwards less
painfully than before either because of the iso-
lation or simply because they help this author in search of

14 × 14

a rhyme around me people study or argue one bloke is showing off
his iPhone 5 and I remember suddenly the good old
days when showing off the first version really made a
splash like suddenly starting to talk bold-
ly in perfect English

                        we're off again this time with a
good *foie de veau* etcetera to aid digestion
that's to say among other things a cheeseboard a
nice bottle of Bordeaux the vague sensation
of being nicely content without pity a-
nd for no particular reason just th-
is feeling of life which is there without pity
and without any particular reason camped out there in th-
e duvet of the girl who's really striki-
ng wrapped up in her fur coat at
my side her mouth made up perhaps her bloke likes that
when he gets horny

                        and then the mystery of why they
put so few sockets for recharging your laptop etcetera
on the TGVs which are alway-
s swarming with workaholics while there are loads in the
new TERs for the bumpkins from the North who
for the most part don't have laptops any more than I
have a tractor and then you might wonder too

why among the few sockets provi-
ded two per carriage for a good what fifty passengers
at least half of them don't even work anyway
it's infuriating at this price one more balls
ache for turbo-profs as well

                                      OK

you keep calm with great tact you negotiate a seat that'
s more cramped than a duck's arse in the train's bureaucrat-
ic space in front of a comfortably
seated geek tapping away furiously on his quiet-
ly flashing PC with its 3G SFR internet key
then can't you believe it he beds down like some complete
twat snug and comfortable on his lit-
tle banquette the electric socket still in use

                                        oh God

shit shit and triple shit in fact fuck it
they've just told us that for an indefinite period
probably as long as a Sunday in the country
the last Paris/Lille train will be further d-
elayed until 22h 21 for Christ's sake fucki-
ng get a move on SNCF please before I end
up cracking up completely and hand in
my season ticket

14 × 14

                    around the same time the train
pulls off moving slowly through the
night and I read what I'm in the middle of writing
reflected sideways white on black in the
mirror of the window meanwhile a bunch of arseholes needing
a fix of r 'n' b creepily take over the
carriage filling it with a steady din
coming from a shared and maladjusted headset the‐
n snap all goes quiet again or almost just the noise of the train
itself an old couple vainly searching for a topic
of conversation and a group of young adult‐
s for whom the total absence of such a topic
of conversation doesn't stop them from rabbit‐
ing on non-stop for a second

                        then at last in the morning a
shiny new TER for Valenciennes packed with e‐
lectrical sockets wherever you look and not a
single user of any kind of portable electrical
appliances (apart from yours truly of course who takes a‐
dvantage of the situation to play a *Fall*
CD and starts to dance inwardly while continuing to write without
even worrying about my various and diverse batteries
for the duration of this journey somewhat
ridiculously characterised by or rather as
"mobile-less" like a journey that's "wheel-less" say

or a day that's "telly-less" though of course nobody
would dare suggest such a thing (I'm on my way
to a workshop where having had the bright ide-
a last week of announcing that
I didn't have a TV one of the kids asked me "but
what on earth do you do then?") the flat
panorama stretches out perfectly on
all sides like a painting only a little spoilt
by the dried streaks of dirty rain
which reflect a pale light greyer than in
reality I imagine looking at the weak sun that
is vainly trying to daub the scene with a differen-
t colour

       and then the return journey in a train without
a single socket at the time of day when student-
s who are at least as weighed down with ant-
i communication devices as I am go back t-
o Lille with their ears more blocked than the sink at
my ex's probably still stuffed as I speak

                            it's the time when t-
ravelling by train (outside dark night deserted betwee-
n the villages and stations) resembles tak-
ing the metro with the same interiority
of passengers lost in their music

or wrapped up in a book or carried away in a
dream each locked in their own world the only
difference tonight is the rain which is bucketing down after a
brief respite forming this time rivers so black that they
voraciously devour the least photon that
might wander here transforming this all into a
fugitive explosion of silver and gold (at the same moment
I play a CD (almost out (shit) the batte-
ry should be OK now) saying to myself it ain't fair
that some groups who I won't name couldn't care
less if they finished off an album
with throwaway tracks without any words whi-
le a writer has only his words to help him
finish a piece off
      another high-
speed train but for the most part going very slowly th-
is time because it's night and around two mill-
imetres of snow are expected what do the
Swedes and the Russians do? but at least there are no chil-
dren thank God (I heard on the radio the other
day that an aeronautical company had started
to offer seats that guaranteed no children under twelve for
all their long-distance flights not a bad id-
ea eh?) just the usual suspects for the morni-
ng the young subscriber to the *Figaro* who cheeky
as a monkey reads my screen looks at me quite

bizarrely and goes off to find another seat before I can
even check the headlines of his piece of shite
(I've the armrest to myself) but there's a problem apparen-
tly coz he comes back soon afterwards
with his paper and his greasy hair which is also covered
with its own particular kind of snow (but has
someone found the head of Henri IV? the question has caused
quite a commotion for it seems that some politician
has been stirring the coals again regarding his intentions which
is all very interesting but hardly compen-
sates for my elbow on the armrest) nearer to Paris switch
there's no snow whatsoever but the train doesn't go any faster for shit
so what can you do nothing (that's it)

The Paris of Clouds

The Paris of clouds
chases the clouds of a wager
of an apparent simplicity
while your wager at the bar
piles up, white, red and yellow
and words chatter on without end

like an eternal city, without end,
the Paris among the clouds
piles up white, red and yellow
you lose your love you lose your wager
in the conversation at the bar
with an evident simplicity

it's so dense, this simplicity,
like an eternal town, without end,
while during a conversation at the bar
the good lord flies off into the clouds
and you lose your bearings you lose your wager
in this light, pallid and yellow

in this glimmer, pallid and yellow
which is so dense, the simplicity

depends on the relative odds and not just on the wager
on a possible existence without end,
the good lord flies off among the clouds
from the other side of the bar

at the other end of the bar
the mouth in the mirror grins yellow
seems lost in the clouds
murmuring that all the simplicity
of a non-existence without end
depends on reasoned odds and not just on a wager

it chases the clouds of a wager
while your wager at the bar
and your words chatter without end
the face in the mirror grins yellow
murmuring that all the simplicity
vanishes, lost among these clouds

At My Place III

Terms of divorce via facebook let's start here
around the table again then calm down again a
bit
    terms to stay with your grey eyes together
though they barely glitter anymore under a
sky which is a bit limp tonight
                        terms to do fuck all
                                      life
with its way of continuing continues to be blunt
like some dumb bird while being shagged
                                your wife
for instance yes you can imagine her yes her cunt
out for the benefit of who some cricket fan
between two pints of Guinness or two whiskies whatever

terms for an abandon you see what this caveman
town where you live like some Jesus in sever-
ance from some good goddess
                            hey this ham sandwich
with mustard but no cornichons (what a bitch)
is still dead good
                and then what do you call a
couple of gays in France it's Frédéric and then

what do you call a woman with one leg shorter tha-
n the other well Eileen of course and then
what do you call a guy with no arms and no legs
swimming in the sea well it's Bob look-
ing at Cliff with a gull on his head
                                        then suddenly the music begs
really to be heard a presence hung on its hook
you casually start to dance like an idiot
just idiotically happy
                        around the table not even
not this time just a glass of vodka a bit
early this but how to put it from the window heaven-
s to Betsy the passers-by are all uglier than
shit especially those of the female persuasion
but love continues and continues a mad obsession
fucking you into some shit blacker yes far more
than all the other shit of varying tones from black
to brown figured by your imagination as raw
as Parma ham
                    then later that evening back
at home why not some rosé while listening
to the BBC talking about a new ceasefire
in the middle east which is fine after taking
in England's cricket team's frankly dire
defeat in India again I mean really this is

14 × 14

starting to get a bit much
                          the table is so what
well filthy in fact yes just quite simply piss-
like the inner part of my desire for a life that
binds man to woman with all that implies I mean
imagine the fuck-up a bit really picture the scene
the radio's now singing love songs all
alone in the void yes quite simply one body
plus another which thus form a third to do fuck all
with such a fleeting life it's a slasher movie
directed by a god along with a devil
with some simply timeless flair if this
has any meaning in this language capable
of everything and nothing it's to make this
pompous like it does with easy stuff
like love quite simply fucking in fact
                                      your
speech starts up again your mouth enough!
saying something tenderly ridiculous as ever
like for example no I won't even say
it out I'd promised this thing that's true one day
that I wasn't going really to speak about your arse
and me in my writings as if you and me
were eternally anonymous in some French farce
with the world spinning right there as it can as though we
had nothing really to do with it nothing at all

before the coffin bearers
                              look if you're thirsty
there's some orange juice to cut your vodka
                                                to call
you out on this do you for instance quite simply
yes you I mean just listen to the radio
for a while like that crap your parents put on
every Sunday while they were doing what I dunno
twiddling with the roast for instance or pardon
fucking in secret or else bawling each other out
like married loud and messy lawyers shout-
ing in front of you (but what filthy fucks they
are the products of all who screw ever onward
apparently in some complete dumb splendour yes totally
like that)
              then to make a break in a word-
less world I cogitated for a while in a kind of void
the lack of matter between two galactic
masses once again while hoping that we'd avoid
saying something dumb your voice funnier than just a tic
that's what and if we talked about the Septaine
far but not that far in fact from Bourges and its way
of quite simply being in fact a blen-
d which is totally strange and weird a display
of irritation and surprises and so on given that
we live in an occupied space i.e. a flat

14 × 14

full of what let's make a short list for ex-
ample (by the way what's a Septaine do you know?
no I suspected as much its residents for ex-
ample don't either) with among other things row-
s of army bases you can't enter you just pass in front
of by car on roads straighter than a finger raised
towards the future where the present you confront
is slightly curved like the butt of a top model upraised
there in front of you while you fall asleep as
politely and as physically and as verbally
as possible then you rub your eyes then as jazz-
y as nature is ugly sometimes you can really
feel that imaginary wind in your nostril-
s as if you were also that slim svelte kestrel
diving bang onto a mouse already panick-
ed by the shadow sketched forever in its dreams
of danger and you too probably coz genetic-
ally of course that's how it goes or so it seems
I mean dumbly playing out total horror
just like pain is an alarm signal often given
really too late to tell you it hurts old fella
so stop where you are but you're already fucked when
that happens whatever but where were we? oh yes
the Septaine and its soldiers' kids who desire like
practically any kid basically undergoing the stress
of a kid's dreaming at least fleetingly to be like

their parents just now or eternally while
later they don't have the slightest clue worthwhile
about some kind of future which takes you along
a route that's in motion but flat too towards
an invisible horizon it's not the moon not a song
you have in your brain no it's the sun onwards
you go seemingly getting closer which is
dumbly blind like a headless Irish turkey who's
looking forward to Xmas like a weird future which is
there inside the head of someone who's
so weird that they're fuller (even more so) than a can
of human sardines or of other species from the sea
in a world where people snuff it from nothing less than
cancers which are statistically caused by the
level of the ambient radioactivity
from the army's tests which have quite simply
not been published publicly the statistic-
s where folk need to get how they lost a loved one
before so to speak digging into this earth so ridic-
ulously anonymous mute and dull in a way (on
purpose I mean it's as if you wanted to
disguise a serial killer as a simple citizen
so to speak) that they're hiding under a look just too
let's put it this way normally dumbly ren-
dered there before you like a village just like an-
other village followed by another like another

village like still another and then there on the left an-
other one again (where we could be lover-
s I reckon either moribund or else fucking each
other's brains out for months on end speech-
less while the grass grows like the grass grows
and the neighbours gossip like neighbours gossip
and the long-dead bakery opens up again glows
interiorly with no flour yet on loving fingers) blip
let's get back to the point cancer firstly that seems
to float in the air like a whiff of vodka
like a lastingly fleetingly mind-fuck love affair or dreams
in a nightclub between a man and a
woman simply there mutually attracted like
two genes already arguing lovingly over the
future of the thing to be created hetero/trans/dike
or why not something else again (scarily
if you truly contemplate real life
imagine the genetic link a husband and wife
linked to others that you couldn't even sketch out
in your dreams (solitary species living probably
in lakes isolated beneath the Antarctic during about
a million years at least without really
any need to mention life on Mars or on some
exoplanet (if we adopt a view taken
from the earth) to evoke a world which is rum
as they say nuts like the beasts living sunken

in the depths of the Pacific Ocean with gaping maw-
s which are pointlessly (apparently) colourful
given the total darkness around them (apparently) draw-
n by a piss-stained artist having drunk a bellyful)
look then at this life that exists which is produced
in a nuclear-loaded world induced
militarily in its denseness where they've called
the café/restaurant right in front of the army base
Dangers (watch out this restaurant has polled
only 20% of positive votes among the race
of web users) which reminds me oddly
enough of the café/restaurant right in front
of the prison in Douai which is blatantly
called *You're Better Off Here Than Opposite* blunt
but true and while the canteen for soldiers
is as disgusting as the equally disgusting one
which is inflicted everywhere on our poor juniors
so much so that they must end up thinking that even a bun
at school must have been genetically
modified compared to the one simply
served up at home on a plate that has by various lives
and chance been cracked (unless both of them
come down to the same thing) here by the wives
of soldiers left on their own while their gem-
s of hubbies do mysteriously secret stuff
in Yemen for instance or elsewhere

14 × 14

in countries where the Chinese are known enough
to now seem rather omnipresent yeah
it's almost like the rabbits in the fields
of the Septaine while starving kestrels
glide in the air whose azure somehow shields
us from a sun that seems ever lower which tells
of an optical illusion right from your memory
like in a childhood garden a flower you now see

And You

and you your voice
bewitches me you see
like your fingers

and me my body
bewitches you I see
more than death

we linger
how we linger
one against the other like two fingers

and me my voice
spellbinds you you see
like my fingers

and you your body
spellbinds me I see
far more than death

14 × 14

we linger
how we linger
one against the other
like two fingers

cut off
from
reality

Whichever the Café

In any old bar I mean there where you plant
your butt for a few minutes waiting for a train for
instance waiting to be hungry or a girl whatever let's rant
about what for instance sales figures or sex for
instance get chatting about whatever why not
indeed your sex life why not indeed
that interests everyone or practically the knot
between one another and vice versa is so fluid
and absurd that what happens between the sheets
becomes so fascinating for one another that
the poor cunts we are sitting there in front of Jeez
nothing just a glass of white wine a flat
beer for instance which then becomes something
a bit less lousy
                      look over there at that dribbling
idiot staring into his future just like
a pigeon with a broken wing looking like a loon
at a car as it speeds up
                                   here nothing's gonna be strik-
ing except for a stolen motor for instance
                                            the moon
takes on a strangely familiar appearance like

14 × 14

you between two sulks or else two elderly lovers
                                            a hairy
fuck-face with a dumb nocturnal look that's what he's like
your guy who I hunted down on the web really
no totally stupid as I am so serves me right God
gifted me with such a big nose like a lousy snoop

silence flees like a wallflower like a stupid sod
flees the love of his life then curls up in his coffin-like coop
while the world continues to spin around just
like a poet around a metaphor or a man must
around meaning and definitely not the love
of his life like a dog also turns so as to flatten
quite stupidly and calmly before lying above
the virtual grass of an ancestral prairie when
not yet civilised guinea pigs scampered
not yet in their dreams and where men dressed in
fatigues now shoot birdies
                            right now I'm unhampered
about ideas of going home before starting one more in-
credible philosophical conversation about
tax rates in France for instance for instan-
ce and so on
                several days later you go out
fatter and dumber than ever eyes lower than
your belly or your balls and the world seems so wei-

rdly familiar and strange that you almost wee-
p in your pants so what
                         then just where you are
the silence hugs you like the limp arms of a cheap whore
pretty of course but who keeps coming on far
too much about making you come just like more
or less any girl in fact what incredible thera-
peutic insistence which is seeming-
ly just about universally female a
given no I mean it's like they're all coming
on insulted about their desirability or else power
while the opposite sexually is rarely true as though
masculine pride were set in an non-ivory tower
stocked with easily shared things such as so
to speak a pack of fags for instance or else a bo-
ttle of rosé just set there and being rather autistic blo-
cked in shit like a girl sulking at Christmas
because her sister has a finer gift than her
(or which was more expensive no real fuss
about its subjective qualities)
                               water
is a little-known element around here seemingly
to judge by the contents of the glasses
around here but also the hazy look apparently
projected by the regulars like grime from arses
onto the porcelain and other china thing-

s stuck by filth to the walls thus defying the most
basic physical laws of the universe like nothing
entropy for instance or else gravity a ghost
thus resulting while the surrounding chat
turns even dumber like this prat
talking about the hopes in Marseille this Saturday
to gun down gay marriages I mean seriously
can't they just fucking leave us all alone *non mais*
and just live out their lives like lonely
gits we're not in England after all
                                            and then
the day "without your cell" doesn't seem to be
working among these rustic homophobic men
with their fat fingers nor by the lycée you can see
through the window
                                        neither that much in Fives where
people are as thirsty as usual it would seem
without giving a tuppeny fuck about each other
while shaking their fat hands over a dream
a beer and a joke which ain't obscene enough to be
funny then the big misty mirror allowing the
barman to get a broad view of the café (just in case
something really interesting might have occurred
for once (dream on you fools and pace
the booze (and what is written (on the blurred
mirror of course) "SEVICE (i.e. Torture) AU BAR" in bright

pink letters))) while the radio is talking to
itself reeling out inaudible news between light
pieces of totally unlistenable music who-
se only role seems to be to increase the
sound level thus forcing the drinkers to
yell even louder
                      mint tea
and espressos now just to change the mood feeling blue
as you are lingering in the grains of other co-
fees almost drunk and the green leaves that wallow
still in their light brown fluid
                             or else when-
ever while right here in Saint Pol the petite bourgeoisie
round off their unnameable meals this noon then
go off to do their jobs like soft sleazy
fuckers as limp as their chips and bland as their supposedly
spicy sauces but decidedly a bit greenish
at least for the moment and marshmallow-like clearly
fatty and sticking to your gut
                                  then feeling sheepish
trying to wear yourself out this time in the local bar
which has now been miraculously repainted
into a kind of filthy nicotine tinge so far-
fetched that you'd ask God if it existed
and thought about such things (sometimes I wander
around thoughts of such things) right up in the wonder-

land of its great solitude what explanation it could see
compared to my little version of a life
discretely distinct from others that's it maybe
a gesture towards ciggies without strife
which in principle only yellow your own
insides with the butts filling up
the little iron bucket by the door while people moan
about a possible fine that never hap-
pens really except after a miracle or a whistleblower
who spoke to me in another bar where they smoke openly
(as opposed to the one just beside it where not a
single drinker dares smoke while the walls are totally
covered by photos of puffers from the past
in the very same bar by a pro (yeah he was a blast
I was told) and sure enough they are really
neat (it's a face fuck like putting snap-
s of naked girls on the wall blatantly
in front of guys who can't screw no more)) crap
shut up for now I set off home to find my gra-
tin dauphinois and while a frustrated smoker by
the bar can't even swallow his Leffe anymore a-
fflicted as he is by all the snot in his guts ri-
sing o tempera o mores (things were better
before innit?)
                      at the Café des Sports (with view
over the Boucherie Amazigh "Stuffed Lamb (guts gutter-

ed quite clearly) Brochettes and Merguez" a non-Jew
is speaking a particularly violent dialect
of Arabic into his cell phone direct-
ly rendering inaudible everything else even the radio
the traffic as well then off he goes to pee
but the usual silence of this place takes oh
so long to return and others start to belly-
ache like gas avoiding any danger of a
vacuum while my basic but broad understanding
of languages from right around the world a-
llows me to grasp that they're talking about cars unending-
ly (right here near the border with Belgium
there is what might be termed a little trade which
is alternative (so to speak) my not so dumb
neighbours used to change number plates ditch-
ing the foreign ones while using a drill after they
had stuck on one made of painted cardboard cra-
zy but let's not be too snoopy and shut
up these brackets (and this passage as well
while we're at it))
                          at the Bibliothèque Nat-
ionale the café is probably even more hell-
like than the dives in Fives if that's possible but
you sense vaguely that this has been done on purpose
and not just from clumsiness or lack of ambition but
from a blatant desire to be ugly or chase those

14 × 14

who hang out like a dike with geezers in haste
to hook up with just any bird (and certainly not
with any guys totally spaced and waste-
d out but that's another story) for me not a jot
of hesitation I piss off to finish my beer
sitting comfortably in front of the queer-
ly carted chunk of the forest of Fon-
tainbleau transported by a truck
to be replanted here nice and fresh and com-
pletely daft as a mahogany frying pan
                                         later at the fuck
stupid Rendez-vous des Belges by the Gare du Nord
two slightly "mature" women talk about starting
a group of "cougarettes" first off with the poor
barman while grinning at me not having
drunk just soup these two it seems (me neither but
I know how to stay calm looking at the stuff
on my screen while one asks the other you know what
kind of animal a cougar is I mean daft enough
(so I end up laughing a bit but not really as
much as usual)) then beers down and clad like what was
once a man killer (so to speak) off they go
towards other adventures (phew I can
now finish this poem here or rather no
keep the goal kick for home)

IAN MONK

                              having waited longer than
a cunt for a bus it's here it's over or
nearly so shamelessly right now I'm peering
at you for instance there beautifully draw-
ing languidly on a cigarette yes like going
down on an imaginary dick but think more
about the real dead end once out of here (in
fact I've never seen someone drop dead or
practically so in a bar whereas I've seen
everything else it's sometimes better to go out
quite clearly than booze inside like some homey lout)

14 × 14

If I Were You

If I were you I wouldn't start from here

If I were you if you're having the steak and madam the sole then a dense Rioja would be just perfect

If I were you if you're having the dense Rioja and madam the flighty Chardonnay then a seafood platter would be just perfect

If I were you if you're having the shite Chardonnay and madam the Spanish plonk then panfried squid would be just perfect

If I were you I wouldn't start from here

If I were you if you're having Tokay and madam the Spanish gut rot then the octopus in off-green ink would be just perfect

If I were you if you're having a hard-on and madam the oysters then a chilled San Pellegrino would be just perfect

If I were you if you're having the kidneys and madam her periods then a Luxembourg rosé would be just perfect

If I were you I wouldn't start from here

If I were you if you're feeling suicidal and madam is having the onion soup then a subtle but brutal Chilean red would be just perfect

If I were you if you're having the cheese platter and madam a nervous breakdown then a vintage Burgundy white would be just perfect

If I were you if you're having a thousand-year egg and madam severe diarrhoea then a vigorous Australian red would be just perfect

If I were you I wouldn't start from here

Whatever

The content could be any old shit you just need to fill
in the blank space in other words follow
the thread from a given A to any old B passing the time simul-
taneously for sure even if you spend it all on your ow-
n whatever bang you could be doing anything
at all your index finger stuck up your left nostril
and it carries on even without you lifting your little fin-
ger which comes in handy for scratching your arse who's got the job surel-
y not you who like the morons who say
yes sir no sir without even lifting their middle finger
half an inch and then right there I see
that your ring finger is still without our
wedding ring and that you've put another ring in its place
to conceal precisely the place where the farce
of our marriage stopped the sun from hitting your
finger and so allowed our lamentable history and
our inexistent future to appear
meanwhile outside right in front of our eyes another world
carries on its hangers-on pushing
drugs just a little not too much for certain
stealing likewise flirting likewise fucking
likewise in a dingy room behind torn curtains
beneath flowery sheets dripping with the ghost-

ly memory of other fucks and other bodi-
es given that oh shit the laundromat
is still closed and that I'd rather die
than buy a washing machine no life is too
short finally shit and then the wage so
hard to earn and all for this kind of shite
it's not worth it and above all if it's a matter of In-
come Support mindlessly squandered at Carrefour like
a good housewife and then at the tobacconist's and then
even at the café sometimes well why not it-
's a matter of passing the time which will pass as I've said in any
case but not so quickly you need to face it
life gets reduced to that sometimes no I mean to say
wait that it passes totally mindlessly like
waiting for a bus during a nation-
al strike which ends up arriving all the same like
death and the manner so to speak of waiting so long
depends simply on the amount of
money that one has during this period enough
to be slightly out of it all the time or completely
plastered in any case the other one spends the time
alone or more exactly it seems that he
doesn't move and it's you who move through him
just as the countryside doesn't fly pas-
t beside the train rather it's your
train which flies past beside it then wise as

14 × 14

a dick you take out your finger your thumb from your
various and diverse orifices and decide immediately
to go outside yes why not it's a nice day again
after all your stomach is full your mind empty
like the eyes of the neighbour who's been beaten up again
an arsehole who abuses without
compunction all the same all the same you go out
you go down the stairs the Portuguese on the ground
floor have bust the lock again and strewn their cans o-
ver the pavement like so many killing jokes scattered
there among other empty packets of mashed potato
pistachios for example why not then the inevitable
doggie diarrhoea and vomited pizza goo
you go out then into a sun bizarrely and unashamedly beautiful
yes it's astonishing this sky as blue
as the cheeks of the neighbour her arse too
probably I imagine such a shame no think of something
else for example her and her hands so soft to
the touch for example well that's not bad no not there in
the road otherwise you risk getting an inopportune
hard-on as obstinate as a fan
mindlessly stalking their chosen star
who couldn't give a shit about them obviously well that's just hum-
an isn't it it's a question of hierarchy or
it's inhuman isn't it it's a question of sim-
ple pretention which is human too after all

like it or not for sure we've got nothing to do with humanit-
y when you think about it men and women stroll
around mindlessly right in front of you in the street
like sheep towards what well towards the nearest
supermarket for example Carrefour Market
to be specific where the people happy or long-faced
walk like the condemned towards the check-out
as dumb as anything divesting themselves of their cash like a
wanker clumsily spilling his sperm like a
suicidal wreck spilling his blood in the bath so you go out
and the supermarket eyes you up like that
Brazilian whore doing without
junk while she makes economies so that
the man in her life with the help of plastic surgery
no longer looks too much like her or she like him no
matter in brief you go out to do your shopping ethically
no forget that you buy let's see two
steaks some hot dogs junk food whatever I mean really
fuck the organic section and the like no shit
just forget it just stuff your face like a doggie
lying about in a street without bins you get it
people lapping up pigeon shit and then tucking into more shit
the droppings of . . . who cares don't mention it
you couldn't care about the exact origins of this kind of stuff so
once you get to the super-
market what do you buy why pasta with tomato

sauce to go with it of course and then var-
ious kinds of shit to spread on a baguette
budget price butter for example
rubbish jam but real Nut-
ella because I can't stop myself the full
bust of the cashier almost makes you drop your w-
allet right in front of the boob(s) but you
pull out like a satisfied prick and you go out again as if the w-
orld belonged to you more than anyone else there you
think of the boss of FNAC for ex-
ample who you see but I can't remember his name my ex
again on my phone what a pest she is she
doesn't know when to let it drop and then the car
park is still there in your face like some shiny
inevitability which you swallow up without ar-
gument for the world is like that
yes the world drags its destin-
y ceaselessly and blindly onwards apparent-
ly towards the café opposite where the talk of the town-
's about societal values and the lat-
est football game between Lille an-
d Kronenbourg no I mean Copenhagen yes that's it
I think no matter so another beer man
funny this feeling of being drunk without being
drunk less funny the messed-up face of the other human being
there next to you her nose in her glass of

rosé which is dripping in front of you with blood and
snot (her nose obviously not her glass of
rosé which grows warm on the bar between her misshapen hand-
s with yellow and black nails) so you take a glass
of rosé too no matter to
pass the time and then you realise that time is
getting on and so you leave to
do what to do something else for example let's
have another drink in a less dodgy café but
what'll you have to drink certainly not a rosé let's
see yes a pastis yes why not yes that-
's just what the doctor ordered so as not to want
to throw up all of a sudden but shit what
the hell no let's have another rosé a-
nd then head back that's a promise no question
because of all this effing fresh produce so fresh tha-
t it'll stink to high heaven given a little sun-
light or just sitting in this café hot as one of our hypocrit-
ical love bites head back then on the pavem-
ent you notice what nothing apart from a bin and its mites and shit
and then what now what now oh look two m-
ates over there about to go into the café opposite OK
fuck it go and say hello to them then it can't
do any harm no you decide not to no way
hanging back for a moment it doesn't
matter you scatter your energies and your seed where you can in

14 × 14

the fierce grip of your faithful fingers for example or else slippin-
g between the milky thighs of that one o-
ver there which are clearly less burdened by fidelity
but at the same time clearly more soft to
the touch shit get a grip on your shitty life is just like that apparently
and isn't about to change decisively you
have another drink a Ricard for example yes
why the hell not then slightly the worse for wear you
head back to do what to do whatever Monday is
turning into another abstracted day some-
one should invent a word for days like that you kn-
ow which are all alike but which at the same
time resemble a nothingness so heavy that it becomes unn-
ameable but come on let's go drain your glass
and you head back finally then before your milk turns
and your steaks go rotten in your shoppi-
ng bag for the fridge must be filled like a
day or like a life in general to get down to the nitty-
gritty there are the mites that jump out and a
rotten apple to boot but look at the yoghurts going in
and the fresh juicy steaks that'll end up well sometimes
at least in the crapper after a good meal washed down
with rosé or not it all depends
on the state of your guts or they might go str-
aight into the bin for non-recyclables
that's to say all the shit of one kind and another

which is fine for when you think about it shit is
the most recyclable thing in the world so you
sit down in front of the telly which is telling you
what it's telling you that the Islamic extremists are burning
down all the cinemas meanwhile in France the
times of national pride are again
in the ascendancy but what rotten luck our tetra-
plegic handball team have been
thrashed by the Chinese in London or something
along those lines no matter so just kill time
as best you can with another the gorgeous thing
who's also ugly sometimes and sometimes just
like you too but you couldn't care less you just want to
cross this page of space-time and get on to the next
one it's finished or nearly yes nearly yes completely idio-
tically just like that yes going from A to B
like this dictionary scarcely opened in front of me

14 × 14

Songs of Reflections

the songs of reflections in the glass
prolong the night of memory
and the evening of beer and whisky
the girls and boys turn pale one and all
one in front of the other the other in front of the one
in the mirror of desire

in the manor house of desire
ice cubes swim in polished glass
the alcohol stronger than the one
unforgettable night of memory
the girls and boys trapped one and all
in reflections of whisky

and in the stench of whisky
there still glimmers a kind of desire
unknown to you unknown to all
the ice melts in the glass
wherein drowns the memory
of alcohol longer than one

of your myriad reflections of one
month without a thought without whisky

wherein drowns his memory
where there still glimmers a kind of desire
a just-flickering flame for this icy glass
familiar to you familiar to all

will shut tight little by little on us all
on his reflection the one
permanently fixed in the glass
a month without distinction in the whisky
in the night of desire
and the hell of memory

then the hell of memory
is drowned little by little in us all
without the night of desire
one after the other the other after the one
in the hall of beers without whisky
echoes of songs and reflections in the glass

Relative Redundancy

. . . love
. . . and then
. . . shove
. . . again

I'm trying to say she loves me so
and then the next day shit
she says no
forget it
she talks about all this like a stubborn cunt and says she has to go
good riddance there's no point wondering why
no
point making a song and dance about it

                                                    you try
to rebuild your life and this life isn't going too badly up until the day you
       come across Camille or mayb-
e it's Dominique no matter a babe
whatever your kind
of girl friendly
kind
cheeky
like you

yes that's it
like you
but
a bit more what's the word "styled"
no sexy
a bit wild
you flexi-
ng in her arms which are thinner by
far than her fingers
                        eagles fly
across the valley
as if there
was nobody
here
below like you or me
crossing the road on our own like grown-ups but yes
with difficulty actually
yes we scuttle about like legless
cripples with such a physical connection to the sky
a bit too much like eagles in fact

wanna cry
but
don't do it fight
it like a grown-up like a real bloke right
for a change

and no longer like some queer mother
while you have derange-
d me and others
down there and so on
no longer know what we want
or even don't wan-
t your mouth full of shit like a cunt
like an overflowing cup

wanna shut up again
otherwise I'll crack up
then
nothing
at all nothing
of nothing at
all
except
well
quite
stupidly
love right
(how daft is that he
thinks) to
find meaning in
well life and you
there you thin-

k about what right
about the bloke who for example might
make you
come
or might not but make you
become
wet yes or just a bit for starter-
s then no good
and then the choice fact according to a BBC reporter
during a programme about food
and poverty
that people prefer
pizza to broccoli
well we can only concur
nothing to
be done in any case
                       they're all going to
die
faces drunk with melted cheese
the dough barely
risen not even an anchovy for the wise
amateurs when it comes to capers and
olives and pimento
they prefer dishwater or something bland
to
Mariage Frères tea

it's the scoop of the century don't you know it
(especially
if we spice it up a bit)

now it's hailing in a sticky
and not very
convincing way like a gently persistent rain
completely soaking
you again
like a thousand miniscule detumescing cocks falling
from the good lord himself
                              it's absurd-
ly wet and clammy on your neck like the slime of a slug
snapped up by a blackbird
besmirching its yellow beak
                              it's bug-
ging in the end isn't it
this feeling which buries you in
icy coldness like a shit
in
Cling-
film with a zing
like that of
a fresh corpse laid out on a bier
or on the cold marble of
your dreams as stiff as you are here

the cold penetrates
the flat
insinuates
itself between the door and the carpet
gently separating
the
crumbling
bricks the mortar and the
cement light the oven
the door open
put your feet in front of it so that your toes
turn marble-pink with an almost unbearable

pain the bottle of lukewarm ros-
é is drunk the table
stares at you blindly
its reflections empty of sense then
only the bills remain obstinately
to be ignored again
as long as possible
outside
the sky invisible
void
you sleep fists clenched
on two patches of sky wrenched
from the interstellar void

while on the ground
the bangers carry on schizoid
going around and around
you sleep or try to at least without conviction
eyes staring at nothing dead beat
the phantom
                      empty eyes the pallid complexion
of your childhood comes back to haunt you replete
with all the bad vibes and your
own kids are sleeping
now in the gay and pure
knowledge of sleep enclosing
like this their nightmares
right here under the stairs
snug at their parents' while you lie
wake up suddenly with a shout
mouth dry
belly turned inside-out
burning and retching bloody yellowish bile

and then outside the world
starts up again why why not with a smile
quickly gets going like a feeding-tube suddenly unfurled
and plunged straight into the oesophagus you know
how it rages along without a snag
without apparent sense as stubborn as the antlers which grow

on the head of a stag
without apparent sense except pure show
otherwise know-
n as genetic investment
in apparent uselessness to stun
the feminine or masculine sex a bit like your poetical achievement
for example like football-like silicon
or like a suicidal attempt to impress some initiates

and then outside the moon
scatters and laminates
all the reliefs of the town
with a negligent and borrowed luminosity
while the snow again
starts to slowly
fall like rain
so beautiful
so mortal-
ly virginal under
your shoes
full of holes which take in water
between your toes
made numb
with hooch and cold
overcome
as if amputated anaesthetised old

14 × 14

patiently awaiting the surgeon
one more time always
no it's not urgen-
t just love one of these days
then
again

[3]*Forget It Never Mind (2)*

forget it when I say get lost
forget it when I say I love you
the moment's not right this evening
the moment eludes us tonight
the room shrinks into us
the room welcomes one and all

the thing welcomes one and all
and so I repeat get lost
the thing boils down to us
and so I repeat I love you
today here now tonight
here right away if you want this evening

here right away if you want come
the thing shows us the way
today here at once right now
and so I repeat just a half barman
the thing boils down to this
and so I repeat right

[3] So:

then you hold me right
and you say come
finding out like this
a possible way
we say just a half barman
a half for God's sake right now

a half for God's sake for the day after tomorrow
then you hold me tight on the road
we say this will end badly
and you say give it another whirl
whatever life throws up
in stumbling blindly towards death

forget it when I say death
the moment eludes us for the day after tomorrow
the moment's not right life throws up
the room opens on the road
the room spins another whirl
forget it when I say this will end badly

The End

So the end starts here before going the
extra mile into what well you're used to it
I guess in whatever hell direction
                                    you see
words are self-sufficient sometimes
                            who cares
                                        the litt-
le world suffices unto itself to suggest one end
among other potential conclusions
                            who care-
s meanwhile you need to do something tend
your looks for instance to be prettier then prepare
some pasta to remain alive a bit and right
after that grab a jacket neither too plain nor grubby to stroll
warm and dry beneath the moon
                                and no I don't have a light
and no ciggies either and you're really droll
but not tonight Josephine never again in fact and I'll
be keeping my cash for myself
                                then shit and brown bile
do you probe your eternal imaginary soul
on your sleeve each time you set foot out of doors?

the end for instance being I can't find my hole
which is precisely the end while everyone snores
on their feet yeah you and me both so we've become
just two shadows in a now closed café
having turned into just another lousy store some
place where we drunk to our futures with no aim we
went on endlessly then while outside the moon was
refracted in the otherwise invisible drops of this
fine and incessant Lille drizzle as
I gathered myself by taking in my absurdly short yellowis-
h tongue while with your head lowered
you crossed the street and bellowed
like a recently released demon in this world of cowardly
virtuous cunts
                       in fact I don't believe really
in ends not at all in principle nor in lovely
beginnings either no more philosophically
than poetically being as I am on a quest for forms that
can at least theoretically be propagated
from both the bottom and top towards infinity that
form of space time according to Buddhism not related
to the given moment when it started but
prolonging the past indefinitely
(just as it does for Europeans into the future with nut-
ty versions with hells or heavens clearly
still alive and kicking despite everything)

but oddly enough not in this book of sing-
songs you're holding in your hand which is head-
ing straight towards its beautiful end planned from the start
just like you and me though unconsciously dead
as sure as in any so-called piece of art
which is in reality directed by
one little ego which is both as suicidal
and galloping as cancer or else why
not a particularly Ebola-like virus one and all
being massacred so fast that its bearers don't even
have enough time to pass it on to others and
even less to reproduce themselves
                                        so even-
ly paced from one clubfoot to another and
so on the whole business advances with no need or
desire to look at its own traces nor
seeing in your creepy eyes the proto-palimpsest
of its own end
                    what else to say? what to say in any case?
and how to hide a certain haste to test
out an experience of the void gaping in your face
in a growing dilation just ready to give birth
to a black hole as gleaming as a pussy?
                                        tonight
the street for instance tomorrow the café your berth
whatever nowhere mainly see you later right?

14 × 14

whatever happens anyhow
                                    tonight the bed but also
the ceiling attractively yellowed by the strip
of streetlamps being diffused by the snow
like eyes tinged with cirrhosis rheumy at the tip
of a nose of gaudy zigzags going to a mouth that ooze-
s more than this snow reduced to a soup by the shoes
of sliding drunkards on a track while zigzagging
back probably where to? who knows
nowt before the thaw tomorrow morning

fuck it let's have a bit of fun anything goes
like a drink it's now or never after a blood test
which by God knows what miracle a-
nnounced that you still have the liver of a baby your best
vieille prune followed by half a bottle of vodka
and in the end everything seems more impossibly
distant than ever like a *mise en abyme*
following all the rules of perspective so thoroughly
classic they're unbeatable (except maybe in a dream)
another night the same bed again and the same light
an attack of jaundice usually white-
r than rampant anaemia in daylight while by
the bed or to be more precise the mattress
placed on the floor the plaster fuck knows why
is starting to swell little by little making a mess

of the paint forming pink veins and patche-
s scattered around as though on a gouty foot
thus clearly contrasting with the thick moustache
of dust topping the skirting board
                                          hard put
to getting out of here before it's too late how about
going for a coffee downstairs? who
wants a game of pool before I bomb out
financially and the end of time comes, like an ado?
who wants me quite simply hey you for ex-
ample? why? my conversation? like my ex
girlfriends who still like me well enough though
it's all over between us I mean really? nonetheless
who wants nothing in the end? who's become hollow
rather wise a bit zen-like with the aim of emptiness
fitting us like a luxury coffin? and then who
wants some more samsara like a good tulku preaching
his crazy wisdom around a good bottle of who
cares in fact (while not still presupposing
that some Rinpoche or other who (as opposed to
the stem cells (infinitely divisibly
immortal) that make him up remain to-
tally imbued with the potentially
empty permanence of his own integral
nature)) but look at what isn't at all full
in fact let's go and have a drink some place

else and quick about it I mean faster than
the jerk of my very own id (so face
it I don't give a fuck how this makes a man
's life run aridly (so to speak) towards an infinite
(perhaps) soup more diluted than one served up
in a global deconcentration camp set just right
at 0° K (or perhaps not let's keep it a bit up-
beat and go for the critical mass supposed
for an eternal cycle of bangs and crunches
thus explaining *inter alia* the frieze of juxtaposed
existences (thanks to those apparent free lunches
(despite the bill remaining to be paid
later on)) reincarnation or the feeling made
quite simply by a vague sense of déjà
vu which would be caused just by the coming
together of the same particles same place on a
scale containing a quantity literally humming
with undefinable smiles coming from all the point-
s of departure and analogous arrival (I did say
say that we were going for a drink in the joint
downstairs didn't I unless it's too late already hey
look they're chucking out the passing pissheads so
we're fucked already unless we knock on the backdoor
before they throw out all the regulars also
(do you reckon that life if you get me has more
or less regular souls just like the ca-

fé downstairs while others seem to pa-
ss by just once in this infinitude of ex-
istences and which then makes all that
tip over once and for all (unless there could be a "nex-
t time" as you'd put it)? (chat it's all just chat
so what about thirst then? I'm fucking parched me)
(but the discourse keeps winging away
like a migrating goose on Dexedrine but whose destiny
(polar or temperate that all depends) is delay-
ed perpetually remaining just as distant at
the same speed as its approach) (what about
the beer and a game of the pool while we're at
it?) you already heard the last shutter no doubt
about it as it went down and the farewells (maybe
(why not)) echoing in a sonorous void now re-
constituted like every evening around them so it's
fucked quite clearly so let's calm down and take it
in instead of making a French cheese stink of this
anyway what's left at worst there's always a git-
like bottle of Chuche Mourette (a gift almost forgotten
from whom knows who or why the fuck (to be
rid of it presumably)) which has been going rotten
in its sugar and the cupboard for at least three
or four years but it will serve its purpose
let's hope as both a vomitive to block
this discourse and a laxative for each of us

adding our own colour variations (knock
on wood we won't internally create a total
inner vacuum setting off as a result physical-
ly the implosion of the person in question who
will thus end their life as a microscopic black
arsehole falling into the water of their own loo
a smaller splash than you'd have wanted back
when you started out limping foot after limp-
ing foot on this potentially beaten path already
twisting ankle after ankle with not even any simp-
le respect for your body (geometrically
speaking of course) on your way towards (

) a blank oh
well you get up in the day after's endless-
ness having fallen flat onto another life's tomorrow
now she's run off laughing like a fucker in the rain
that way for instance yes exactly that way again

By the Sea

we mingle at last
to start a life
with its ten fingers
a goddamn stiff
typed out flat for you to see
amid a dance of drinks

among these drunks
we mingle at last
falling flat for all to see
and so create life
modelling a stiff
with our own fingers

like your finger
in a world that's drunk
modelling our own stiff
let's chatter at last
just about life
dead, sketched out by the sea

"Wherever", "At My Place I", "On the Lille Metro", "At My Place II", "At My Place III", "Whichever the Café" and "The End" translated by Ian Monk. All other translations by Philip Terry. "Listen Out", in English and French in the original edition, is reprinted without change, as is "If I Were You" which was written in English.

IAN MONK was born in London and is now based in Paris, France. He is the author of numerous books (mostly in French, some in English) and has also translated a large number of authors (Perec, Roussel, Le Tellier . . .). He has been a member of the Oulipo since 1998. This is the first time a full collection of his French poetry has appeared in an English translation.

PHILIP TERRY was born in Belfast, and is a poet, translator, and writer of fiction. *The Penguin Book of Oulipo*, which he edited, was published in Penguin Modern Classics in 2020, and Carcanet published his edition of Jean-Luc Champerret's *The Lascaux Notebooks*, the first ever anthology of Ice Age poetry, in 2022.

www.ingramcontent.com/pod-product-compliance
Lightning Source LLC
Chambersburg PA
CBHW031321160426
43196CB00007B/615